Postcard of coal miners taking a break in a Russell County, Virginia coal mine, 1926. The man in the center is Frank Kilgore, "Papaw" of this book's author.

Author's Tribute: Papaw Kilgore worked 43 years hand-drilling, hand-loading, and hand-pushing thousands of tons of coal out of a very dark and dangerous environment, day in and day out. He lost many friends and members of his extended family along the way. Many miners died or were permanently mangled, mostly in violent and sudden fashions. Their fellow miners attended the funerals, helped the survivors best they could, and went right back into the mines. PTSD was not known of then but it took its toll nonetheless.

The coal that Papaw (and hundreds of thousands of miners like him) produced helped fuel local and nationwide businesses and the rest was shipped around the globe. Millions of Americans burned coal to keep warm, heat bath water and cook. At that time in the USA, and most other countries, the mining of various minerals was the world's most dangerous occupation. All that Papaw knew was that he was feeding his family and, in a small way, fueling the rapid growth of his country and other, hopefully friendly, nations. He was humble, quiet, kind-hearted and never started a ruckus.

My hero never drove a car. He walked a six mile roundtrip each day (except most Sundays) to and from the mines, sometimes "doubling back" another shift because Appalachian coal was in such demand. He supported his family of nine in a three-room coal-heated house. Along with his passel of kids he raised corn, cows, hogs and work horses on very steep hillsides and tended a big vegetable garden on what was considered "flat plots" in those days.

Papaw died a gasping death from pneumoconiosis, a fancy name for black lung disease. He was actually luckier than most miners; when he retired he could still walk without slumping or hobbling, despite suffering many joint mangling mining accidents. Toward the end he "piddled around the house" best he could. I loved him and he loved me, despite my rowdy ways.

Coal miners do America's dirty work. They and their predecessors deserve America's respect.

J. D. Vance Is a Fake Hillbilly:
Think Twice Before Calling (All) Coalfield Appalachians Racists, Sexists, and Ignoramuses

Cover photo: The 1951 state champion Norton, Virginia, integrated Little league team boarding a plane to play the West Virginia champion team. This coalfield town fielded the first integrated team in the south.

Published by Fake Hillbilly Publishing
www.FakeHillbillyPublishing.com

Book and cover design copyright © 2022 by Fake Hillbilly Publishing

ISBN-13: 978-1-7333644-0-9
Large Print ISBN-13: 978-1-7333644-1-6
Hardcover ISBN-13: 978-1-7333644-2-3

Merchants and non-profit groups wishing to sell this book may qualify for discounted pricing. Also, if a reader finds a grammatical error or factual mistake please feel free to email info@FakeHillbillyPublishing.com.

To my children, Joyce and Jason, no matter what few hard assets I have gained after decades of hard work, none of it would be worthwhile without the joy and challenges of fatherhood.
You all make my heart sing. Love you.

This book is also dedicated to all people who have struggled to achieve the American Dream and came from far away with nothing but hope and a willingness to work hard. Most of our forefathers and mothers would today be classified as "underdogs," and that is how the United States of America came to be. Unfortunately, many of our ancestors, while seeking a better life, also created underdogs along that journey. Many humans were

slaughtered to make way for expansion, or were enslaved to make life easier for the more affluent.

That is our country's history and literally the history of the human race as we all evolve and learn, sometimes painfully learning the same lessons over and over again. Hate is easy. Being objective and empathetic is apparently very difficult.

J.D. VANCE IS A FAKE HILLBILLY

THINK TWICE BEFORE CALLING (ALL)
COALFIELD APPALACHIANS RACISTS, SEXISTS,
AND IGNORAMUSES

FRANK KILGORE

FAKE HILLBILLY PUBLISHING

CONTENTS

ACKNOWLEDGMENTS

Thanks to all my friends and family members that reviewed the many, many drafts of this book, or claimed to do so. A special shout-out to Proal Heartwell, a Charlottesville native who came to our mountains in the 1970s to help implement the federal surface mining laws that guard our mountains and coalfield residents from abuse and neglect. He is the co-founder of the Village School for Girls (and tomorrow's leaders) grades 5-8. His edits were precise, plentiful, and very much appreciated. It would take another book to quote Proal's Banacek truisms that I naively try to live by. One in particular baffled me until a late-night epiphany: "When an owl comes to a mouse picnic, he is not there for the sack race." That's Socrates stuff.

And a big thanks to Jim Branscome, a legendary reporter for the *Washington Post* back in the day. He gave me a taste of journalism at an early age by writing an article about my penchant for eating road-killed groundhogs. I thought it was a confidential discussion among fellow mountaineers. For that, I had him review this book draft over and over and over. My revenge is glutted. I forgive him now, nearly fifty years later.

Lastly, if there are actionable mistakes in this book, Jim did it.

1

A REAL MOUNTAINEER'S CHALLENGE TO J.D. VANCE

Let all decent Appalachian residents say it clearly: J.D. Vance, at the tender age of thirty-two, had no business writing the elegy of Appalachia. Whether or not it is pretentious to write memoirs at that station in life depends upon that person's accomplishments and ego (Malala Yousafzai of Pakistan he is not). For J.D. to speak for an entire region was way over the top, especially given his intermittent and very narrow exposure to our Appalachian region, culture, and history.

His very limited view of a region populated by twenty-five million or so Americans living in 420 counties spanning thirteen states could not have come at a worse time. If kicking a wounded dog while it is attempting to stand back up is fun, he must have had a blast.

What he did accomplish is setting back several years of strenuous efforts to transform the coal mining region of the world's most ancient mountains from a mostly natural resource extraction economy to one with a sustainable mix of tech jobs, tourism, advanced manufacturing, and higher education.

Despite a half-century of hard work toward reshaping our coal-fields economy and breaking loose from very harmful stereotypes perpetuated by an elite media, J.D. took up the defamation flag and stuck it to us with gusto.

This young traumatized man kneecapped some very serious efforts at economic recovery in Appalachia by providing excuses to the far right not to waste money on such a hopeless place and gifting fodder to radicals on the far left by excusing and reinforcing their longtime sniggering stereotypes of us. Simply put, J.D. gave culture bigots a chance to crow.

His book was a wholesale ultra-negative categorization of an entire population. This gave elitists like Bette Midler the opportunity to set aside her "inclusiveness" gene and say this about an entire state because its U.S. Senator, Joe Manchin, dared to be a moderate: "He sold us out. He wants us all to be like his state, West Virginia. Poor, illiterate, and strung out."

History will reflect that Senator Manchin, a mountain politician that has common sense (and, just as importantly, can add and subtract) likely saved our nation from a full-bore depression so that we can instead wallow in an inflation-fed, budget-busting recession for the next several years.

Fighting unnecessary wars on the credit card, bailing out crooked Wall Street companies and dropping money from the sky over the last few decades have taken their toll; we simply cannot keep printing money with reckless abandon (my bad, we more and more just send funny money onto computer screens as if digital debt means we never have to pay up, apparently all the government has to do his hit "delete").

As far as vilifying Joe Manchin goes, if both sides of the aisle would stop up-staging each other just to arouse voters the best parts of the Build Back Better (BBB) proposals could have been adopted years, if not decades, ago and helped millions of Americans gain access to essential services. Instead, each political party thinks that when they have a majority they can shove bad, self-serving legislation down the throats of the other party and the voters that support them. Assuming that they have a slam dunk in hand the more greedy legislators slather a good bill with pork fat until its original intent is lost. Then, occasionally, one or more bi-partisan members say "no" and the fat gets trimmed or the winner take all crowd gets nothing, thereby setting back the much needed portions of the legislation for years.

As mature humans know "all or nothing" is not a smart strategy for success and is plain stupid when the resulting "nothing" hurts real people.

And let's face it, building and renovating roads, bridges, tunnels, water and sewer systems and Internet access are quantifiable, easy-to-see tangible accomplishments. To the contrary, some of the aspirational, difficult to define, quantify, or understand, portions of the original BBB were simply a windfall for perpetual grant recipients who can write fantastic applications but very rarely bring home the bacon because the viability and outcome factors are so amorphous. Accountability matters.

Most Americans understand and supported the infrastructure bill and hopefully support the practical parts of the BBB package that Manchin ultimately supported. For example, the lack of competition now favoring the corporate prescription drug cartels desperately needed to be fixed long ago but legislators, Democrats and Republicans alike, were simply bought off by campaign donations and thinly veiled free junket trips to exotic places.

By the way, Senator Manchin and his West Virginia Republican colleague, Senator Capito, are consistently ranked as two of the most bi-partisan members of the Senate. What a coincidence that West Virginia, the only state almost entirely made up of the Appalachian coalfields, has the best "let's work together for Americans" record in the nation when it comes to its senators.

Another act of environmental hypocrisy is worth noting when it comes to Senator Manchin and his part ownership of a power plant that seems to make Wokes go nuts. In fact, that and other specialized power stations throughout coalfield Appalachia were specifically engineered to get rid of waste coal (GOB) that has polluted our mountain watersheds, waterways and air quality for over a century.

Hundreds of millions of tons of this stuff are constantly degrading coalfield Appalachia's environment. Some geniuses advocate digging up and reburying this methane-leaking junk. This is not feasible because the deeper one buries a mega-mass of organic materials, the more likely they will spontaneously combust and spew 100% pure toxins into the air.

What Manchin haters apparently don't get is that methane, not carbon dioxide, is the most potent source of climate change. Methane doesn't hang out in the atmosphere as long as CO2 but it is the most difficult to control.

According to the EPA and other sources methane gas emissions primarily come from the following sources: natural wetlands, rice paddies, livestock production systems, the burning of wood (including runaway forest fires), landfills, and fossil fuel methane emissions.

In other words, no matter how GOB is buried it and other waste coal will emit methane around the clock. Burning this nasty stuff in low emission power plants is the best recycling tool to get rid of it forever instead of letting it lay on our watersheds and in our creeks for centuries, or catch on fire and pollute the planet after billions of dollars have been spent to landfill massive amounts of organic material. It simply won't work in the long haul.

In addition, how much watershed degradation will occur as the proposed new GOB landfill sites disturb thousands of new acres of surrounding land? And do we really want to drain all wetlands and close down life-sustaining agricultural systems such as rice paddies and the livestock industry? Of course not. Instead we need to concentrate on the most obvious carbon sources of methane leaks and fill them. This will be much easier to do than plugging up flatulence-emitting cows.

The first steps are to get these old coal waste piles permanently cleaned up by incinerating as much of their organic matter as possible and, concurrently, compelling all natural gas companies, distributors and users to pay extra to fund very stringent inspections and controls to reduce the massive leakage problems in the drilling, capping, distribution and user processes. This effort will not suddenly stop climate change but it will be one of the few things we can immediately do to lessen the looming disaster. Until sun, wind, geo-thermal, hydrogen and safe nuclear power can synchronize day in and day out we need to at least pick the low hanging fruit of environmental clean-up. We can't let future generations of humans find out that we fiddled while Rome burned.

So, we have a big GOB problem in Appalachia today because customers of yesteryear enjoyed low cost carbon energy to the detriment of the humans that extracted it and the environment that hosted it. We should all pay the real price as we go and maybe then conserving natural resources might make economic sense to everyone, not just conservationists. (Disclosure, the author in 1977 was designated as Virginia's conservationist of the year for helping adopt federal surface mining controls, a topic referred to in a short story at the end of this book)

Coalfield Appalachians have been living with this nasty GOB scourge for decades and decades because our mountains have been unofficially designated as a national sacrifice zone whose second class residents for way too long just needed to sit down and shut up when it came to mining deaths, mangled bodies, spent lungs and environmental disasters.

I challenge anyone to come up with a better way to rid ourselves of GOB coal, and the methane and leachate it secretes daily—that is funded, feasible—functional and not environmentally harmful in its own sphere. And consumers should stop whining because these costs are tacked onto today's electric bills, that can was kicked down to us by our rootin' tootin' ancestors just as our present population is doing to our children and grand babies in similar situations. The chickens have to roost sometime.

Until then, please stop demonizing the coalfields then having a hissy fit when we are trying to clean up the worst of the mess that resulted from being treated like a third world country for over two centuries. Yes, I said it, third world.

A gob coal pile on fire in West Virginia. Some of these sites have burned for years, spewing unlimited carbon and toxins into the atmosphere

A half-million tons of GOB coal were cleaned out at this one site near the small Virginia coal town named Clinchco. The coal was separated from the rock and dirt, blended with higher grade coal and burned in the nation's lowest omission power plant in the U.S. One could call it recycling, but apparently the critics of Appalachia want us to leave it in the creeks. Yes, that wet area on the lower right is a buried creek.

A century old GOB coal pile after reclamation in Wise County. The waste coal was burned at the same low emission power plant and the blighted area reclaimed.

How DO we resolve the dangerous radicalization of both political parties and work together on these types of urgent matters? This may sound radically moderate, but how about the unaffiliated voters among us flood the primaries and conventions that actually create presidential tickets and ballots for other important people, such as legislators. That is the only way to make sure that the zealots on the fringes of both parties don't frame our future choices.

Literally, if you don't participate in the nomination process then quit griping that you don't like anyone on the November ticket. Outnumbering the radicals on both sides is the only way to bring common sense back into the American political system. The new and reelected level-headed leaders and moderate negotiators could then address gridlock and quash hate-filled partisanship in a productive fashion. Then all Americans win; we are in deep doo-doo otherwise.

But, back to J.D. and Bette, peas in a pod when you think it through.

I have some more sobering news tidbits for Ms. Midler, one of which is that West Virginia ceded from its mother state (that would be Virginia, Bette) because a big majority of that region's "hillbillies" opposed slavery. A month after the United States government recognized this Union stronghold as a new state, the good citizens of Manhattan (where the nation's self-elected Woke Diva resided for decades) turned a war draft resistance demonstration into a riot aimed at Black free men and women.

Over one hundred of these Black Americans died at the hands of a racist Yankee mob simply because they were easy to hate and convenient targets. The rioters even burned down the Colored Orphan Asylum!

Wokes love to dig back centuries to smear today's descendants of wrongdoers. So if charity starts at home, it's time for Manhattan to be on a very hot seat. Perhaps the island's leaders and landowners should trade their borough back to the descendants of the resident Native Americans for beads and trinkets valued at $24.00? That was the value of this fraud-in-the-inducement land grab back in 1626, excluding interest.

Lead the way Bette, and disgorge your millions received from the sale of your spiffy downtown penthouse and gift it to the descendants of these disenfranchised Native Americans. For your convenience in sending your gross proceeds to the rightful owners, I found out (for you) who to send it to: the Nanticoke Lenni-Lenape Tribal Nation. I am also providing the tribe's email address so a wire transfer can be arranged:

NanticokeLenapeTribe@gmail.com

The tribe members have spread across North America since that heinous theft. Luckily, their headquarters are located in nearby New Jersey, which is even more convenient in righting this 396 year old crime. This population of 16,000 tribal members sure could use some Woke financial assistance, and Bette's legacy for voluntary reparation will be forever etched in stone. And if the tribe members are too proud to accept the money, what about the descendants of the 100 murdered Black Americans who died in downtown Manhattan due to the color of their skin? Or, even fairer, splitting it in half to both disenfranchised populations would be acceptable, Bette.

In fairness, even some of Comrade Midler's own ultra-liberal friends bit into her for slurring the impoverished state of West Virginia. They know that but for Hillary Clinton's "deplorables" quote, our nation would have had its first female president, coupled with decidedly less drama.

As for illiteracy, it may surprise ultra-privileged Bette that West Virginia is historically only a couple notches down from California in nationwide public school rankings (sources: World Population Review and wallethub.com). Both states should do much better, but which one has the most financial capacity to rocket to the top? As I recall, the Golden State had the *world's* fifth largest GDP in 2021.

But I digress, Bette needs her own book expose. That is in the works.

What J.D. could (and should) have done, instead of making millions by broadly perpetuating images from his traumatic childhood, is help create worthwhile jobs for our mountain children and grand children. Yet he chose to spout his self-loathing on the talk show circuits to reinforce the images of Li'l Abner, Snuffy Smith, and Jed Clampett (albeit Jed was a really good guy and routinely outfoxed Mr. Drysdale), and other illiterate mountain caricatures that snippety writers took, and still take, great pride in pushing onto naïve audiences.

Just as impoverished city dwellers must tire of being assumed to be drug dealers or takers, gang bangers, natural born killers, and unable to master the English language, so are mountain people sick and tired of being misjudged and ridiculed at will.

At least African-Americans were offended enough to form the NAACP and many other unified counter-punchers. Jewish communities also have their effective anti-defamation leagues to fight bigotry so serious that their people have literally been murdered by the millions simply for existing. Migrant workers also have a sympathetic media and organized groups to push their causes on a daily basis. Yet, native coalfield Appalachians are treated with unfettered disdain. We have a lot in common with these and other distinct cultures in terms of being perpetual underdogs. Hopefully, positive change for all is in the air.

Appalachians, of course, are not the most oppressed population in our great nation by a long shot, but we sure understand that bigotry and slander are the major causes of lack of investments, good jobs, and hope. Who is going to invest in our young, smart people (many of whom would love to remain in, or come back to, their mountain homes) if all potential investors hear is bad-mouth drivel spouted from unlearned sources? Not many.

But the investors—angels or otherwise—that do give us a shot are generally greatly rewarded with affordable labor and land, dedicated employees, and a friendly atmosphere situated in a temperate climate with abundant bio-diversity, fresh water streams, wildlife, outdoor recreation, and some of the most accommodating people on earth.

A sizable working farm can be bought here for the price of one D.C. brownstone. Victims of raging forest fires, merciless hurricanes, killer tornadoes, searing droughts, and dangerous gangs can be safely nestled in the lush greenery we call home.

But back to J.D., he is no more of a "hillbilly" than I am a flatlander. My Scots-Irish family has been in the Appalachian Mountains since 1770, and many of them fought in the Battle of King's Mountain, a turning point in the Revolutionary War according to none other than Thomas Jefferson. Fortunately our coalfield society is wide open to new residents if they come here for the right reasons and with open minds.

So J.D. is not as welcome to call us out as he may think. In fact, his western Ohio home place is "flat as a fritter," and the only common sense advice he ever got was from his Appalachian grandmother who, although very flawed, cared enough to see his potential and urge him to do better than his particularly dysfunctional family.

Had J.D. actually been a student of Appalachia, especially coalfield Appalachia, he may have avoided advancing his bigoted and patronizing slander cloaked as a rock-in-a-sock beating. With a little effort he could have learned how diverse, accepting and colorful his Appalachian maternal coalfield roots really are, before shaming their existence. The boy is clearly into deep root denial.

J.D. may have a law degree from Yale, but I am betting he has never argued a case by himself in any court, or represented poor clients who were up against moneyed opponents. Having no financial ability to attend law school I did it the very old-fashioned way, "reading the law" under a mentor, then passing the Virginia bar exam, one of the toughest in the nation. After all, Thomas Jefferson (again) read law under George Wythe and did okay.

Thereafter I practiced real, down-in-the-trenches law. Just a client and his or her lawyer, against-the-world kind of lawyering. I have tried thousands of cases in the Appalachian mountains since 1982, representing numerous landowners and employees against coal companies; defending the United Mine Workers strikers during the Pittston coal strike of 1989 (3,500 or so strike-related cases); providing due process for hundreds of teachers; and fighting for numerous victims of domestic abuse, serious injuries, and government overreach or underperformance.

So I challenge J.D. to take me on in any talk show that will have us. Just two White guys, one old, weathered, and salty; the other young, pompous, and extremely elitist, and let's see who comes out on top. The subjects will be something very foreign to him, although he made big bucks tearing them down; and those topics are the actual history and culture of coalfield Appalachia. He will learn a lot, respect for real mountaineers being the most important. I am easy to find, J.D., so give me a shout.

In order to not be like J.D., with his sweeping generalizations and all, I am writing mostly about the coalfields of Virginia, where I was born and raised by a World War II crack-shot veteran, coal miner, moonshiner, and bar-room brawler. But I have traveled north and south along curvy mountain roads often enough to know that the Virginia coalfields are a microcosm of the at-large Appalachian coal-producing region with which we share very similar histories, heritages, and cultures.

If a traveler will simply listen, the biggest difference in the various sub-regions of our coal-producing mountain society is fairly simple to figure out: the further north one ventures, the more likely it is that vowels are fully enunciated as we speak. That is pretty much the sum total difference, regardless of race, religion, or politics.

We coalfield American citizens are mostly rural, usually conservative, somewhat libertarian, accommodating to strangers, love our verdant hills and hollers, and tend to be patriotic and family-oriented to a fault. Statistics, successes and failures, and weather patterns differ from northern Alabama to the Pennsylvania/New York state line. Our overall mountain culture is widespread. And yes, just like impoverished communities around the world, we do struggle with poor health, bad choices, drugs, and chronic economic recessions.

This book is not about denial of our human faults and self-inflicted conditions; it's simply an opportunity to point out many of the good aspects of our homeland, culture, and history that go unreported by most of the media and almost every elitist, J.D. being the most galling uppity pontificator of the bunch.

Another irrefutable factoid about J.D.'s little snit-fest of a book says a lot about his devotion to Appalachia. His name recognition for belittling us has motivated many gullible venture capitalists to invest in his efforts to save the heartland. What is the heartland according to J.D.? Here are the **underserved** regions he intends to help with his access to millions of dollars. According to a piece published by Axios, J.D. Vance is "a strong proponent of investing in often-overlooked places," and will use the fund to **"invest in startups in under-served cities such as Salt Lake City, Atlanta, and Raleigh-Durham."**

What is it with this guy? These are *underserved* communities?

Come on back to the Appalachian coalfields, J.D., the place you apparently resent, and we will show you "underserved."

J.D. was once the darling of the liberal talk shows and swoony editors because he reinforced and validated their smear of all Appalachians. It is fairly easy to gauge how un-enamored these pundits are now, particularly after his senate nomination race. The first obvious fissure with the ultra-liberals came *after* his very clever chameleon-like money-making book tour. That is when this media wunderkind tweeted out his self-described title as a "nationalist."

Unlike the cancel crowd, I gave the young feller the benefit of the doubt whether or not he meant he is a White Nationalist OR just a garden variety version, a huge difference. After all, the word "nationalist" ostensibly means putting one's country first. That self-identity is certainly not reserved to only one race, nor should it be offensive on its own as it does not inherently invoke violence. This self-protection tribal attitude, paired frequently with isolationism, actually promotes non-violence by avoiding never ending foreign wars. Unfortunately, like many philosophical political tools, this one has been co-opted by fringe groups for nefarious reasons.

But alas, I was too hasty in giving J.D. a pass; his ultra-pandering senate nomination campaign bid tells the real story of his soul. The radical congressional members he fawned over on the political stage are of the same ilk as Antifa, bitter and ready to heave our nation into a literal and violent civil war. "Winning at all costs" is how dictatorships come to be.

Prior to this nomination spectacle, J.D. was forced from a company board that thankfully invested in a large greenhouse project in Morehead, Kentucky. He, as an individual, called out corporations that boycotted the state of Georgia in protest of its new voter registration laws. Maybe he was trying to earn creds for his future senate run. Or maybe, unlike most pontificators, he has actually read the new voting legislation and decided that one or both sides have exaggerated the issue. I do not know. I haven't read that law so have no opinion either way. But his removal from that board for having a non-violent opinion, even if politically staged, should make us wonder where the First Amendment begins (and ends) and just how long it will take gang-like shaming assailants to seriously erode that freedom.

The similarities between far left and far right radicals are striking. Just like many other holier-than-thou misled revolutionaries throughout history, these toxic participants hate to the nth degree the freedom of opposing thoughts and expressions. As a result, scorched-earth politicians of both major parties have manipulated extreme, cynical, divisive people for a long time, but the past couple of decades seem to be much worse. If keyboard warriors had to reveal their real identity I suspect that online threats and vicious slander would shrink immediately; anonymous commentators are cowards all.

Due to this constant vitriol, millions of Americans hate each other without any apparent reason other than what they think or where they reside. These are the folks that join beastly radical, yet mirrored, violent movements that tear apart the fabric of America. P.T. Barnum got it right about the birth rate of suckers (Google P.T. Barnum, I am showing my age).

Vast numbers of Americans fall for the siren-like talking heads most ready to pump up their preconceived notions about our nation. Wouldn't it be painfully funny if one sadistic but clever basement-dwelling loser is the same voice behind QAnon, Antifa, *and* the Woke movement? That's the only explanation for anyone to cipher how these wild theories co-exist.

So, maybe this comedic wizard is testing just how far and how much claptrap the radical left and radical right can be manipulated into believing, and hold sacred. I envision that each morning he or she dutifully goes to "work" to share the most outlandish idea of the day, thinking all the while that no one on the planet would bite the bait. I am waiting for the next alert that politicians can eat one baby, maybe two under certain circumstance, but more than three is just plain gluttonous. Unfortunately, thousands of followers will embrace the new revelation and immediately force their political candidates to publicly endorse the three baby rule. Even Putin must be impressed and pleased to find out how gullible we are! Or maybe he is funding this divisive farce. Either way, such radicalism weakens America; that we know for certain.

I partially exclude the Woke crowd from the list of violent saboteurs for now, as they occasionally have a few good ideas consistent with our political evolution and are not physically violent as a group.

Actually I am not sure if there is a formal group called "Wokes" and I am reluctant to look. Nonetheless, the Woke movement is being vigorously rejected by most Americans because it seems to be all about over-the-top indignation and extreme hissy fits, but not much substance. However, as long as they stick to keyboards and non-violent word wars that's their right. But the question must be asked: who are these people and how did they get appointed to make up words and phrases we have to accept?

Ironically, the current Woke movement stole the original anti-racist meaning of the word "woke" that arose among Black writers and philosophers almost a century ago. The present "wokeness" of mostly radical affluent White people seized upon the history of this single-issue definition to warp it into an all-encompassing hate of America and its history. As these far left radicals can attest, being mad at history can be an exhausting task.

Maybe Chuck Todd can research and provide us the following stats with this data download: I bet my aging pick-up truck (come on, you assumed I had one) that most Americans of color do not support the far left's hate of their nation and that most White Americans do not support the far right's toxic definition of America. That's why they are called "far left" and "far right" after all.

I have more than once been asked why the Wokes hate Appalachians, particularly us old White guys (OWG), when they claim to be against all racism and bigotry. I assume it's because OWGs are plentiful in the mountains; we usually are not liberal, we love our country, police, military, and flag, and are not particularly open to being scolded and told what to do.

I have a theory that when the most elite of elitists sees an OWG, the first image that pops in their head is being taped-up and thrown into a windowless white van to never be seen again, or they may envision some nut-job loser shooting up a work place. Well, I guess the statistical data backs up those stereotypical assumptions at some infinitesimal percentage level but, like all humans, we should be judged on an individual basis, not automatically lumped in with the crazies among us. Sound familiar?

America's White guys have done several things that are pretty cool, like revolting against England to form the first truly immigrant-based democracy, freeing slaves at a huge cost of White lives, whipping the Nazis and helping save the world, and coming up with ultra-soft bathroom tissues. But our breed also started the slave trade in America and launched many needless wars in the English tradition of nosing into other countries' business. In other words, like all human endeavors, we have a very mixed record.

So here's my reply to the minority of people that nonetheless hate OWGs with what appears to be murderous intent: "Hey, all humans that ever lived, or yet-to-be born, are and will be hypocrites, and, yes, White guys had a 600 year or so run at dominating the Western Hemisphere and invading much of the rest of the world. So, is it time for us to sit back and watch someone else screw things up?" Demographics tend to say yes, but hopefully we will still have the right to vote and be grouchy.

The bottom line is that all Americans have the right to state our opinions as long as we do not promote violence or harm others by outright slander, especially the malicious varieties.

At least maybe now J.D. is finding out what it means to be degraded and marginalized due to very negative presumptions, the kind he threw toward Appalachia at such an inopportune time. If the only goals he had were to make money and gain political status then, to him at least, it was worth bashing his roots.

You see J.D., words and context matter. Let's just call you a pandering, double-speak elitist on steroids for now and not a certified White Nationalist, although you sure hugged up with them during your nomination campaign. To be fair, politicos hug a lot of toxic people they don't exactly embrace (there is a difference) or want as their babysitters, but this embarrassing sham went way too far for any self-respecting American.

Only time will tell if J.D. is personally all-in with these traitors and charlatans, or not. Surely the Appalachian grandmother who obviously loved him, advised the young man to never let anyone take his soul; it's an irreplaceable asset here in the mountains.

J.D. Vance, the sage of Appalachia. (Photo by Dan Sewell, Shutterstock) www.shutterstock.com/license

2

THINK TWICE BEFORE CALLING (ALL) COALFIELD APPALACHIANS RACISTS, SEXISTS, AND IGNORAMUSES

During President Obama's re-election bid, a radio commentator stated with certainty that the conservative "hillbilly firewall" would hinder his election to another term in the states with sizable Appalachian districts. That prediction was not a compliment to our mountain region on many fronts, but it did indicate that the negative stereotyping of mountain residents appears to be the last politically correct bigotry promoted by many segments of the media and elite societies.

The coalfield region of the infamous "Hillbilly Firewall" is shown below:

And the relatively small coalfield region of Virginia is depicted in this map:

Not that facts should get in the way of news commentators' pithy slurs, but perhaps we can use the coalfields of Virginia as a potential case-in-point and counterweight to such bigotry.

For example, the small coal mining city of Norton, Virginia, started an integrated four-team Little League program in 1951, the first such program in the entire South. Charlottesville's team won the eastern title and its handlers demanded that the Black Norton players be taken off the team before the state title game commenced. Norton, having the only Little League program in western Virginia, made the state finals by default. Consequently, no one knew how this brand-new team would play against an experienced program.

Ironically, 1951 was also the year that the University of Virginia's Board of Visitors in Charlottesville was taken to court for preventing a Black student from entering the elite hallways of its very elite law school. The University of Virginia (UVA) at that time was "unwoke", to say the least.

Gregory Swanson had all of the qualifications for admission except the color of his skin. He was represented by none other than Thurgood Marshall, a future titan of the U.S. Supreme Court and one of the most respected jurists that ever lived. UVA lost on appeal and Gregory made history. Despite his legal victory, he did not feel welcome to live on campus and was roundly ostracized; this shunned and obviously determined young man ended up leaving Jefferson's school early and went on to finish his law studies elsewhere.

To this day UVA's law school spin masters deny that Gregory Swanson was the target of ostracization, much less racism. Denying history is a new national fad.

Meanwhile, Norton's Little League sponsors and coaches refused to eject their Black players and would have won the state title by forfeiture had the segregated team failed to show. Instead, Charlottesville came to Norton to pummel the mixed-race upstarts, and lost 12-3. The game was preceded by a Main Street parade attended by 1,400 local supporters, Black and White alike, pulling together.

Only in Hollywood and the Appalachian coalfields could this epic underdog victory have happened in that very widespread racist era.

The first photo below is of the team sponsored by the Norton Lion's Club, and the next picture catches the state champion team boarding what was likely their first airplane ride. The Black players, Harold Mitchell and Johnny Blair, are survived by six of their White teammates as of 2022. The Blue Ridge PBS of Roanoke, Virginia, is filming a documentary of the team at my urging.

So coalfield Virginia became the first locality in the entire South to embrace players of color—think about that. It is high time for our nation to hear stories of Appalachia other than chronic distress, desperation, and destitution.

Norton Lion's Club sponsored team

Norton's state championship Little League Team on its way to play the West Virginia state champions.

Author's Note: For more about Norton's 1951 championship team, including a historic marker dedicated in June of 2022, visit www. nortonva.gov/531/1951-Norton-Little-League-Teams.

More than a decade earlier, in neighboring Russell County, Virginia, the 1938-39 Dante Central High School football team became the first public high school in the *nation* to integrate sports (if a thorough Google search is considered reliable evidence).

Dante (pronounced "Daint" locally) was a built-from-scratch unincorporated coal town replete with a coal-fired power plant, public water system, brand new housing, a company general store, cafés, movie house, schools, and churches, all provided by the Clinchfield Coal Company.

Interestingly, and a prime example of out-of-state speculators buying Appalachian coal property Stilson Hutchins, the founder of the *Washington Post*, purchased 4,000 acres in that region for $18.00 per acre. After failing miserably at coal mining, he sold out to an experienced Virginia investor, George Lafayette Carter, who went on to create thousands of coal and railroading jobs throughout Southwest Virginia and nearby West Virginia.

The housing in Dante (and most Appalachian coal company towns) was separated by coal companies so that Black sharecroppers from the South, as well as Italian, Slovak, Hungarian, Greek and other immigrants, could live in their own mini-neighborhoods within this overall very diverse community of 3,500 men, women, and children. The public schools were indeed segregated by state law. Yet, the coalfields offered many opportunities for these impoverished sharecroppers and immigrants not available in most of the nation.

Coal companies had various motives for separating the races and nationalities from the predominantly White Appalachian native population throughout the coalfield towns and camps. Some company bosses feared that the residents would clash, and others did not want union efforts to gain a foothold; therefore, a separated community seemed like a good defense. Most company speculators, owners and officials came from northern environs where natural or politically arranged settlement patterns in their cities ended up being segregated.

Nonetheless, the coalfield camps and towns were small enough and the houses close enough to promote contact among diverse neighbors. This close proximity worked well for strong inter-relationships and unionizing.

Integrated Dante High School Football Team, 1938-39.

Seagon Hollow, 1916

The town of Dante image above with the hand-printed title "colored town" is on the face of a 1916 *real photo* postcard. The company gave this section of town the formal name of Seagon Hollow, but according to elders long passed on, the town residents, both White and Black, preferred the nicknames Sawmill Hollow or Colored Town.

The term "Colored Town" is awkward to repeat nowadays but, just like the NAACP of today, the historical names of people, places, and things should be considered in juxtaposition to what was accepted at the time, not necessarily by today's ever-changing standards.

The second floor of the two-story church building shown in the postcard hosted a school for the sharecroppers' children and grandchildren until a new brick school, named Arty-Lee, was built a few decades later. The coal company officials in Dante resided in much larger houses on Roanoke Hill, snidely referred to by locals, again White and Black, as "snob knob."

One theory as to how White and Black miners and their families got along so well is that their wages, particularly in unionized companies, were basically the same pay for the same work and experience.

Dante school teacher and her students, 1940. (Note the pride and love in her face)

Downtown Dante, 1930s

Clinchfield Inn, Dante

The Company Store

A 1930s typical native Appalachian coalfield "farm"

In fact, coal town Black and immigrant residents usually had better housing and amenities than many native Whites as represented in the photo above.

Native coalfield Whites usually bought or inherited land, albeit steep and thin-soiled, outside of coal towns and camps. This allowed subsistence farming that minimally fed their families during routine lay-offs and union recruitment efforts that prompted some coal companies to blackball union sympathizers. Many native mountaineers preferred "town life" and abandoned their hardscrabble ancestral farmsteads to become part of a thriving multi-racial, multi-cultural, and multi-faceted community.

As for better wages, Dr. Ronald Lewis of West Virginia University points out that a Black sharecropper in the 1920s was paid once a year and averaged 75 cents to one dollar a day working and living on southern farms. In comparison, while working in the Appalachian coalfields they and their native and immigrant co-workers averaged

$3.20 to $7.40 per day for an 8-hour shift, depending upon skills and experience.

Imagine the allure of 300-700 percent pay raises, new houses with indoor plumbing, and a much greater freedom of association. Coal company labor recruiters went to great lengths to seek and retain experienced miners from Western and Eastern Europe as well as unskilled workers from the South.

This equity of wages was not the custom of the day for African-Americans and certain immigrant industrial and service workers in other parts of America, Irish and Italian peoples specifically coming to mind.

This "equal pay for equal work" tendency in the coalfields provided financial parity and dignity to immigrants and Black miners alike, at least within their own homes and communities.

3

WE'RE MORE MULTI-RACIAL THAN YOU MAY THINK!
THE MELUNGEONS

Other people of diverse racial and cultural roots have lived in Appalachia since the mid-1700s, mainly in the coalfield regions of Tennessee, Virginia, West Virginia, and Kentucky. They are referred to as Melungeons, and for centuries their origins were quite a mystery until modern DNA technology partially settled the debate.

Some theorists, including many people of Melungeon descent, have previously opined that this dark complexioned and unique mixed-race Appalachian population emanated from Portuguese forays into very early America. Another theory holds that they are descendants of Turkish prisoners of war left behind by Spanish merchants. Others speculated that they emerged from Jewish origins, including the Lost Tribes of Israel. However, for eons the most popular local theory was, and still lingers, that they are Whites mixed with Cherokee and other Native American tribes.

The highest concentration of these mysterious mountain citizens is in the Clinch River Valley, with its headwaters in Tazewell County, Virginia. This famously bio-diverse river courses southwest through Northeast Tennessee to the Tennessee River and beyond.

Ironically, some Cherokee scholars also believe that their tribe's DNA includes Jewish blood, and even DNA testing has not completely settled that theory. According to National Geographic, testing in 2013 indicated markers of Middle Eastern blood among some Native Americans. Various proponents of this Jewish lineage theory even speculate that King Solomon may have reached what is now America during his three-year trading voyages to bring back gold and exotic animals.

Many Melungeon bloodlines, according to multiple DNA projects, are made up of more than two races and researchers categorize this fascinating population as a tri-racial-isolate group. Prior to DNA markers being identified, everything about their history was hotly debated, even how they came to be called Melungeons.

The name itself may have first been applied by a Frenchman attempting to start a French Settlement in Virginia, west of the Clinch River in 1791. Francois Pierre Tubeuf was having difficulties with squatters of dark complexions on his huge new estate. Clearly, they were not Native American; otherwise, Pierre would have likely lost his scalp. He is said to have referred to the mixed-race residents on his land as *mélange*, meaning "mix" in French. So, it is plausible that, given his struggles with the English language, he resorted to this French term to indicate that his tormentors were of a mixed race.

However, the more likely theory is that the name came from the Portuguese language, given that Portugal was an early slave-trading country that hired African mercenaries (and alleged cannibals) to abduct thousands of men, women, and children in Angola and surrounding tribal lands on the west coast of Africa. That may explain why many generations of Melungeons claimed to be of Portuguese descent since that was their African ancestors' last place of residence prior to being shipped to the New World.

A more thorough thesis of that history is found in an article entitled "MALUNGU: The African Origin of the American Melungeons," written by Tim Hashaw. This 2001 publication is accessible online at *Eclectic Magazine*, which earns its name for scouting out unique authors and topics. It is a fascinating story of Black freemen having much more portability and citizen rights than the actual slaves that came afterwards, particularly in Virginia.

Many coal counties in the four states mentioned above have long-standing settlements of Melungeons going back to at least the mid-1700s. They usually situated their communities in the least farmable and most remote places in the mountains. There are several reasons for this tendency: the mountainous sparsely populated land was much more affordable and available to a racially diverse group that had been held back by racist state laws and poverty; they desired to live amongst their own kind in isolated places for support and protection (tribalism); and they shared the fear that their potential African blood would cause even more discrimination. It is just as feasible that the Melungeons themselves were not certain of their various racial lineages.

It is written that Eastern Virginia slave runners would sometimes kidnap Melungeon children born of freeman parents to sell to plantation owners. If so, no fear on earth could match that sin. So it was that freed people of color and other minorities came by foot or wagon to the Appalachian frontier for cheap land, job opportunities, protection and social freedom. Occasionally these treks were also motivated by moderate-to-severe brushes with the law.

The non-coal counties of Hancock and Hawkins are located in the mountains of Northeast Tennessee, and are well known for having the largest populations of Melungeon bloodlines in the nation. Their offspring and other relatives were spread throughout the coalfield mountains as they pressed, or were pressed, ever westward into Appalachia's most remote venues. DNA results show that these mysterious Americans are mostly of European and African descent and not so much Native Americans or Middle Easterners, as has been posited by a variety of authors.

The regional claim by thousands of Appalachian people to be part Native American (particularly Cherokee) was likely an attempt to avoid the restrictions foisted upon bi-racial people by state laws before, during, and after the Civil War.

Early 1900s multi-racial Appalachian families:

A scholarly article documenting the influx of sharecroppers to the coalfields culture was written in 1989 by Dr. Lewis entitled "From Peasant to Proletarian: The Migration of Southern Blacks to the Central Appalachian Coalfields." It is a must-read, fortunately accompanied by the following multi-state comparative census chart:

BLACK POPULATION OF CENTRAL APPALACHIA
1860–1980

	Kentucky	Tennessee	Virginia	West Virginia	Totals
1860	5,814	2,175	3,405	3,769	15,163
1870	4,941	2,254	3,885	3,280	14,360
1880	6,734	2,570	4,242	5,781	19,327
1890	7,444	3,653	6,552	12,577	30,226
1900	7,602	3,609	7,056	21,584	39,851
1910	10,222	4,415	7,669	41,945	64,251
1920	15,692	2,943	8,953	60,488	88,076
1930	18,286	2,129	7,616	80,841	108,872
1940	18,662	1,918	7,709	85,465	113,754
1950	14,284	2,941	6,659	86,421	110,305
1960	10,240	2,884	4,083	64,613	81,820
1970	7,232	2,718	2,585	44,956	57,491
1980	6,506	3,253	2,688	42,277	54,724

SOURCE: U. S. Bureau of the Census, *Characteristics of the Population* for the decennial censuses of 1860 through and including 1980. For the counties included in central Appalachia see note 5.

This population tally does not identify people of Melungeon descent as Black or any race other than White. In fact, the current demographic statistics of Hawkins and Hancock counties in Tennessee make no mention of their mixed racial make-up which, if accurately counted, would likely prove that a bi- and tri-racial majority resides there, instead of the official count of 97% White.

Overnight the Appalachian counties having large generational populations of Melungeons as embedded citizens could rival per capita most U.S. rural jurisdictions and numerous cities regarding racial diversity.

https://www.loc.gov/pictures/item/2006677596/ The most notable persons of allegedly Melungeon descent are Abraham Lincoln and Elvis (no last name needed).

In this decade of the "Woke" movement, surely these overlooked Appalachians, dating back more than three centuries, should be celebrated as part of our nation's overall heritage so they can finally come out of the cold. Employment and educational opportunities for their progeny would be greatly, and deservedly, enhanced.

Unfortunately—because most Melungeons are politically conservative—many liberal legislators and influencers that strongly advocate inclusion and social justice will ignore this opportunity to actually make a quantifiable difference.

From my decades of personal experience working with, representing, and studying the ever-changing theories of the origins of the Melungeon people, it is worth noting that in the coalfields, our citizens of Melungeon descent were treated more liberally and fairly than those living in the mostly timbering and farming communities further to the east.

Since their arrival to the coalfields many have held, and presently hold, elective offices and are generational leaders in every aspect of coalfield society. Working together in the region's biggest (and historically the world's most dangerous) extractive industry and sharing those experiences and collective struggles, including a close labor-related brotherhood, garnered many positive and inclusive effects.

Cultural and racial diversity in the coalfields was so embedded that early 1900s issues of the *United Mine Workers of America* (UMWA) *Journal* spread union news in three language sections: English, Italian, and Slovak.

This "melting pot" throughout coalfield Appalachia rivaled New York City and San Francisco in the varieties of diverse populations and proportions. Membership in the UMWA peaked at nearly one million miners during that era. Blacks and immigrants, and their progeny, were some of the most dedicated members and supporters of the union.

Imagine coming from a sharecropping family living in abject poverty replete with shanties and little access to education, medical care, and respect. Or, ponder the immigrants whose first wave of settlers could not speak or write English. For example, a century ago a huge underground methane gas explosion near Pocahontas, Virginia, killed so many recently employed immigrant miners that their grave markers were inscribed in their native languages.

After some acclimation, the progeny of these risk-takers found much greater freedom of association, a strong union, and a better quality of life. By working side by side with White natives, they also forged bonds of brotherhood and community relationships.

Cemetery in Pocahontas, Virginia

Cemetery in Pocahontas, Virginia

In the 1920s, Wise County, Virginia, at 46,500 residents (8% African-American), was the second most populated county in the entire state. The county's 1928 school board summary report below shows the rapid increase of population during the most accelerated coal boom days and the growing number of foreign-born citizens settling in for new opportunities.

The following immigration statistic is somewhat misleading regarding the total numbers of nationalities present, in that their American-born children were (appropriately) counted as White population natives. It's a given that the large family households of that era likely had multiple times more children in their households than their immigrant parents' numbers indicate.

Children and grandchildren born of these early-century migrants increased in numbers substantially until the 1950s, when coal mining automation forced a mass exodus of natives and non-natives alike. Tens of thousands were laid off (approximately one-third of the coal mining labor workforce), and the working-age heads of households, with families in tow, "headed" to the steel mills and automobile factories "up north."

Foreign-born

The foreign-born white population in Wise County for 1920 is distributed as follows:

Country	Number
Armenia	5
Austria	32
Canada	18
Czeho-slovaki	1
Denmark	1
England	34
France	1
Germany	16
Greece	6
Hungary	396
Ireland	8
Italy	107
Netherlands	2
Poland	73
Russia	28
Scotland	9
Sweden	3
Switzerland	1
Syria	27
Wales	3
All other countries	7

Death Rates in Wise County (1913-1926)

Year	Per 1,000 Total Population	Per 1,000 Total Population	Per 1,000 Total Population
1913	14.4	14.0	19.6
1914	12.3	11.5	21.1
1915	10.0	9.5	15.9
1916	12.7	12.7	
1917	13.2	13.1	
1918	15.0		
1919	12.7		
1920	13.4	12.9	19.7
1921	11.4	11.0	16.4
1922	10.2	9.7	16.0
1923	12.5	11.5	24.1
1924	10.9	10.2	18.3
1925	9.66	9.29	13.86
1926	10.42	9.92	16.0
Average	12.05	11.27	18.09

VITAL STATISTICS

II

Birth Rates in Wise County (1913-1926)

Year	Per 1,000 Total Population	Per 1,000 Total Population	Per 1,000 Total Population
1913	42.4	47.3	20.8
1914	40.1	41.5	44.6
1915	37.8	39.2	21.9
1916	34.4	40.8	23.1
1917	38.7	39.5	27.0
1918	30.2		
1919	41.9		
1920	40.8	42.4	23.6
1921	48.1	49.6	32.1
1922	40.6	41.9	24.7
1923	45.1	45.9	35.4
1924	43.0	44.4	27.5
1925	35.34	36.75	19.54
1926	31.91	33.06	19.11
Average	39.31	41.85	26.60

Marriages and Divorces in Wise County (1918-1926)

Year	Total Number of Marriages	Total White Marriages	Total Colored Marriages	Total Number Divorces	Number Marriages to each Divorce
1918	520	362	158	58	8.97
1919	634	488	145	105	6.04
1920	660	503	157	89	7.42
1921	555	441	114	95	5.84
1922	553	437	116	65	8.50
1923	660	534	126	80	8.25
1924	426	373	53	59	7.22
1925	407	341	66	66	6.17
1926	481	408	73	57	8.44
Average	544	431	112	74	7.42

Information about residents of Wise County from 1913 to 1926.

1920 Hungarian funeral, Preacher Creek, Wise County, Virginia

So, it is not clear whether the integrated Norton Little League and Dante football teams were unlikely social experiments, a matter of temporary necessity, or that it was just locally accepted that young Black students (whose schools did not field such teams at the time) simply wanted to play baseball and tackle football with their White coal-town buddies. What is certain is that the teammates' fathers worked closely together in very tight quarters and dangerous conditions.

Maybe the unique coalfields spirit of inclusiveness arose from the logic of survival, in that it was simply not a good idea to hate, or be hated by, the miner next to you who might be, in a flash, called upon to save your life from the various gruesome ways one can die underground.

In those days (and for decades prior to and afterwards), tens of thousands of miners each year were killed or permanently disabled by rock falls, methane gas explosions, underground flooding, electrocutions, and equipment failures. Though rare, miners working at the face of a coal seam could collapse in a split second from asphyxiation as the 200-million-year-old exposed carbon literally sucked the oxygen from the immediate mine interior, a terrifying condition known as "black damp."

If these traumatic events didn't take a miner out of service and into poverty, ever-present chronic black lung disease caused by inhaling coal and rock dust awaited, guaranteeing a miserable, lingering, premature demise via "smothering to death."

Cherry Mine Disaster, RPPC, 259 Miners and Trapper Boys died in that fire. Cherry, Illinois, 1909. Courtesy of Earl Dotter.

Coal mining was one of the most deadly occupations in the nation until enhanced federal safety laws, adopted in 1969, improved the health and safety of miners who were previously endangered by very weak national and state safety standards. Prior attempts to save lives and limbs were too often dictated by coal company influence rather than practical, humane considerations.

As an example of the slow evolution of coal mine safety, the first federal control of coal mining was passed in 1891. In a huge leap for the time, children under the age of twelve could no longer work in the mines within the U.S. Territories.

Fraternal organizations, such as the Loyal Order of Moose (circa 1888), financially assisted their fellow injured miners (or their survivors). The companies and individual coal states oftentimes lagged behind these private humanitarian efforts until the federal government finally stepped in, with gusto, eighty years later.

Contrary to assumptions, Appalachia was not the first region in the nation to produce commercial coal. That title goes to the relatively small coal-bearing areas of Richmond, Virginia, as captioned below:

> The small Midlothian coal field was valuable to the local market, and was exported to Caribbean islands. The coal was valued for its ability to provide heat, and reportedly was used in the White House fireplaces when Thomas Jefferson was president. More than coal brought out of Midlothian, the James River and Appomattox River waterpower was a greater factor in the development of manufacturing at Richmond and Petersburg.[4]

37 men were killed in the 1882 explosion of a Midlothian coal mine, after methane accumulated in the poorly-ventilated tunnels
Source: Virginia Commonwealth University, James Branch Cabell Library, The fatal explosion at the Midlothian Coal Mine

Coal was also mined in Henrico County, west of Richmond.

TABLE 6.07 Coal Mining History: 1761 to 1924				
Name	Origin	Date Closed	Depth (in feet)	General Location
Carbon Hill District				
Saunders Shaft	Early 1800s	1902	220	Near intersection of Lauderdale Dr. and Causeway Dr.
Eureka Shaft	1853	Unknown	230	Near intersection of Lauderdale Dr. and Francis Drake Dr.
Turpius Colliery, Magruder Pit, Maggi Pit	Pre-Civil War	Unknown	Unknown	West of Poplar Forest Dr.
Gayton Shaft, Coke Shaft, Orchard Shaft, Twin Shaft, Double Shaft, Breaker Shaft	Pre-1819	1901	325	SW of intersection of Gayton Rd. and Ridgefield Pkwy.
Edge Hill Shaft	Around 1842	Unknown	264	Near intersection of Poplar Forest Dr. and Taft Pl.
Barbershop Shaft, Railroad Shaft	Unknown	Unknown	Unknown	Near intersection of Gayton Rd. and Milhaven Dr.
Deep Shaft, Air or Shelter Air Shaft, Snead's Shaft, Crouch and Snead's Shaft, Crouche's Pits, Brooks Shaft	Around 1851	1875	200	SE of intersection of Lauderdale Dr. and Westshire Ln.
Coalbrook Slope, Trent Slope, Jos. R. Anderson and Company Mine, Carbon Hill Mine, Old Dominion Development Co. No. 1 Mine, Mule Shaft, Engine Shaft	Around 1848	1903	over 300	SW of intersection of Lauderdale Dr. and John Rolfe Pkwy.
Cottrell's Pits	Around 1835	1841	Unknown	South of Coalbrook Slope
Deep Run District				
Deep Run Pits, Springfield Pits, Duvall's Pits, Burton's Pits, Roxx and Curry Pits, Barr's Pits	Pre-1761	1924	Unknown	NW of intersection of W. Broad St. and Gaskins Rd.

Decades before present day mining became highly mechanized, the equipment used came in many forms and unsafe varieties, such as the wooden-wheeled cart shown below, used to haul coal from the mines to a rudimentary tipple. These homemade do-it-yourself solutions were common in the smaller mining operations. While showing some ingenuity, the equipment designers were obviously not particularly worried about safety. A more "modern" (circa 1940s) version of a coal tipple is shown as well:

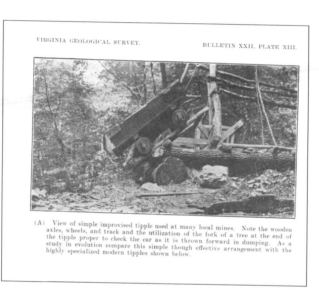

VIRGINIA GEOLOGICAL SURVEY.

BULLETIN XXII. PLATE XIII.

(A) View of simple improvised tipple used at many local mines. Note the wooden axles, wheels, and track and the utilization of the fork of a tree at the end of the tipple proper to check the car as it is thrown forward in dumping. As a study in evolution compare this simple though effective arrangement with the highly specialized modern tipples shown below.

(B) Tipple and loading track of the Hamlin Coal Company at Hamlin, Va.

40

Coal Mining Death Count

Year	Miners	Fatalities	Year	Miners	Fatalities	Year	Miners	Fatalities	Year	Miners	Fatalities
1900	448,581	1,489	1930	644,006	2,063	1960	189,679	325	1990	168,625	66
1901	485,544	1,574	1931	589,705	1,463	1961	167,568	294	1991	158,677	61
1902	518,197	1,724	1932	527,623	1,207	1962	161,286	289	1992	153,128	55
1903	566,260	1,926	1933	523,182	1,064	1963	157,126	284	1993	141,183	47
1904	593,693	1,995	1934	566,426	1,226	1964	150,761	242	1994	143,645	45
1905	626,045	2,232	1935	565,202	1,242	1965	148,734	259	1995	132,111	47
1906	640,780	2,138	1936	584,582	1,342	1966	145,244	233	1996	126,451	39
1907	680,492	3,242	1937	589,856	1,413	1967	139,312	222	1997	126,429	30
1908	690,438	2,445	1938	541,528	1,105	1968	134,467	311	1998	122,083	29
1909	666,552	2,642	1939	539,375	1,078	1969	133,302	203	1999	114,489	35
1910	725,030	2,821	1940	533,267	1,388	1970	144,480	260	2000	108,098	38
1911	728,348	2,656	1941	546,692	1,266	1971	142,108	181	2001	114,458	42
1912	722,662	2,419	1942	530,861	1,471	1972	162,207	156	2002	110,966	28
1913	747,644	2,785	1943	486,516	1,451	1973	151,892	132	2003	104,824	30
1914	763,185	2,454	1944	453,937	1,298	1974	182,274	133	2004	108,734	28
1915	734,008	2,269	1945	437,921	1,068	1975	224,412	155	2005	116,436	23
1916	720,971	2,226	1946	463,079	968	1976	221,255	141	2006	122,975	47
1917	757,317	2,696	1947	490,356	1,158	1977	237,506	139	2007	122,936	34
1918	762,426	2,580	1948	507,333	999	1978	255,588	106	2008	133,828	30
1919	776,569	2,323	1949	485,306	585	1979	260,429	144	2009	134,089	18
1920	784,621	2,272	1950	483,239	643	1980	253,007	133	2010	135,500	48
1921	823,253	1,995	1951	441,905	785	1981	249,738	153	2011	143,437	20
1922	844,807	1,984	1952	401,329	548	1982	241,454	122	2012	137,650	20
1923	862,536	2,462	1953	351,126	461	1983	200,199	70	2013	123,259	20
1924	779,613	2,402	1954	283,705	396	1984	208,160	125	2014	116,010	16
1925	748,805	2,518	1955	260,089	420	1985	197,049	68	2015	102,804	12
1926	759,033	2,234	1956	260,285	448	1986	185,167	89	2016	81,485	8
1927	759,177	2,231	1957	254,725	478	1987	172,780	63	2017	82,843	15
1928	682,831	2,176	1958	224,890	358	1988	166,278	53	2018	82,699	12
1929	654,494	2,187	1959	203,597	293	1989	164,929	68	2019	81,361	12

Approximately 100,000 coal miners died in the United States in the 20th Century alone. Note that fatalities decreased significantly following implementation of the 1969 federal safety guidelines as indicated above.

4

WOMEN AND OTHER INNOVATORS

In addition to racial and ethnic minorities, women also earned opportunities and benefited from coalfield open-mindedness. Even before the Virginia coalfields definitively broke the color barrier in Dante and Norton, Helen Timmons Henderson became one of the first of two women to win seats to the state legislature in 1923. This long overdue civil right came about three years after the 19th Amendment to the U.S. Constitution allowed over half of the nation's adult population to vote.

Helen and her husband helped establish the Baptist Mountain School in Buchanan County, one of the most prolific coal-producing counties in the state. She was nominated to run again but passed away before the election. Her daughter, Helen Ruth Henderson, succeeded her late mother and worked tirelessly for better education and roads for her adopted mountain homeland.

Not only did coalfield voters elect two women legislators within one decade, but both ladies were "outsiders" from Missouri. These elections should also debunk our reputation for hating outsiders. (Alert! The novel and movie *Deliverance* are not documentaries.)

These elected female officials got things done and were much loved and respected due to their unbridled devotion to children, education, and improved transportation.

Helen Timmons Henderson

Mrs. Walter Colquitt Fain, left and Mrs. Robert Anderson Henderson, first women to be elected to the Virginia General Assembly.
—Photo by Staff Photographer.

First Women Elected To General Assembly Guests At Reception

Norfolk Pays Homage To Her Own Mrs. Fain And To Mrs. Henderson, of Southwest Virginina, On Eve of Their Departure For Richmond.

Speaking of supporting women, during the state's 246-year history only six females have been elected to the Supreme Court of Virginia by the Virginia General Assembly. Interestingly, three of them (yes, half) are from coalfield Virginia, and each had as her primary sponsor Delegate Terry Kilgore, a Scott County Republican farm boy and the most recent majority leader of the Virginia House of Delegates.

Cynthia Kinser of Lee County stands as the first and only woman to become a Chief Justice of the Court. Although this dearth of female justices is an abomination, the three coalfield women members of that Court come from Virginia's last frontier and the heartland of the so-called "hillbilly firewall."

Not bad considering the extremely small population in the mountains compared to the state's more thriving communities.

Left to right: Now retired Justices Elizabeth McClanahan and Cynthia Kinser, and then court of appeals Judge Teresa Chafin, from the coalfield counties of Buchanan, Lee, and Russell, respectively.

Justice McClanahan subsequently served as the dean of the Appalachian School of Law in her native Buchanan County, an institution that I was honored to help establish. (Disclosure: the author is the proud spouse of Justice Chafin who worked her way up the ranks from juvenile court, the circuit trial court, court of appeals and now the Supreme Court of Virginia.)

Speaking of the Appalachian School of Law, it might be a surprise, or more likely a shock, to the nation's negative notions of our region to learn that it consistently has the most diverse law school student body in the state, as the photo and stats below demonstrate:

Faculty and Staff of the Appalachian School of Law

	1L Students	2L Students	3L Students	Overall Student Body
Diversity Statistics for Appalachian School of Law October 2019				
White	43/72 (59.72%)	33/43 (76.74%)	30/49 (61.22%)	106/164 (64.63%)
Black	7/72 (9.72%)	2/43 (4.65%)	11/49 (22.45%)	20/164 (12.20%)
Hispanic	10/72 (13.89%)	0/43 (0%)	3/49 (6.12%)	13/164 (7.93%)
Asian	3/72 (4.17%)	4/43 (9.30%)	2/49 (4.08%)	9/164 (5.49%)
American Indian	3/72 (4.17%)	1/43 (2.33%)	1/49 (2.04%)	5/164 (3.05%)
Non-Resident Alien	3/72 (4.17%)	0/43 (0%)	0/49 (0%)	3/164 (1.83%)
Unknown	3/72 (4.17%)	3/43 (6.98%)	2/49 (4.08%)	8/164 (4.88%)
Non-White	23/72 (31.94%)	7/43 (16.28%)	17/49 (34.69%)	47/164 (28.66%)

Appalachian School of Law
White: 69.2%
Black: 12.3%
Hispanic: 4.1%
Asian: 5.5%

Marshall-Wythe School of Law
White: 75.8%
Black: 6.7%
Hispanic: 4.2%
Asian: 3.9%

Antonin Scalia Law School
White: 74.8%
Black: 2.0%
Hispanic: 7.7%
Asian: 7.2%

Washington & Lee University
White: 75.3%
Black: 5.1%
Hispanic: 4.5%
Asian: 6.8%

University of Richmond School of Law
White: 73.5%
Black: 6.6%
Hispanic: 1.3%
Asian: 3.2%

Regent University School of Law
White: 75.7%
Black: 7.2%
Hispanic: 7.2%
Asian: 3.2%

Liberty University School of Law
White: 75.8%
Black: 4.8%
Hispanic: 6.8%
Asian: 3.2%

University of Virginia School of Law
White: 74%
Black: 5.7%
Hispanic: 5.2%
Asian: 6.8%

*All statistics are from American Bar Association disclosures and can be found on:
http://www.abarequireddisclosures.org/Disclosure509.aspx

If readers are surprised, and I hope better informed, by this list of "firsts" found in just our little corner of the Appalachian coalfields that is true progress.

But wait, I have another gem to share regarding the Virginia coal-fields. The Slemp family has a 172 year history of coalfield-bred public service. From the state legislature, office of presidential secretary, the U.S. Congress and now, Charles "Chuck" Slemp, the Chief Deputy Virginia Attorney General, this generational family of patriots has made our coalfield heritage shine.

Campbell Slemp held a state legislative seat as a Democrat, then switched to the more progressive Republican Party due to Democrat autocratic and racist policies. In 1902 he won a seat in the U.S. Congress, the state's only Republican member at the time.

His son, C. Bascom, succeeded him and was the only Virginia Congressman to support the 19th Amendment to the U.S. Constitution—the law of the land that eventually allowed women to vote. Every member of the state's Democrat delegation voted no. Some sources claim that he was the only pro-women congressional vote in the entire South. Hopefully that is not accurate.

This is proof "beyond a reasonable doubt" that coalfields residents march to a different drum in all realms of fairness, especially when compared to many parts of the nation. Even today we elect pragmatic state legislators to send to Richmond in the Slemp tradition.

My great Uncle Wilse told me one time that he liked his politicians the way he liked his steaks, medium. We proudly send firefighters, not flamethrowers, to the state capitol.

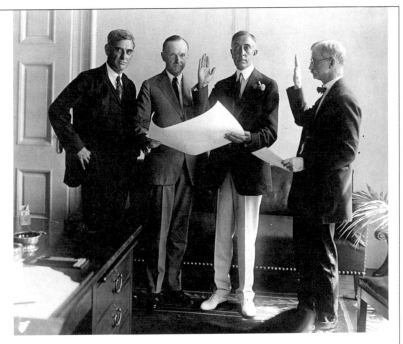

President Calvin Coolidge (second from left) swearing in C. Bascom Slemp (second from right) as his presidential secretary in 1923. Courtesy of Library of Congress.

Did we have and do we have glaring exceptions to these standouts? Of course we do. But being consistently denigrated for centuries for our alleged stupidity and closed-mindedness is based upon ingrained bias and overt lies. By the way, much of the progressive movement talked about today started here, in coalfield Appalachia.

Despite this long history of inclusion, I am many times called upon to account for racism and sexism in the coalfields by my friends from other sections of the state and "up north." I point out, a little defensively I admit, that although Virginia's coal towns and camps were indeed racially segregated, the races and immigrants in most Appalachian mining communities shopped alongside each other, ate where they chose, went to the same movie houses, worked side-by-side in very dangerous conditions every day, and belonged to the same union.

As a self-appointed coalfield historian and an alleged mountain ambassador-of-sorts, I dutifully provide whoever will listen with examples of our egalitarian and independent culture.

One particular fact is that before coal was commercially mined region wide, in what is now called coalfield Appalachia, our ancestors represented a sizable pro-Union sentiment before and during the Civil War. This pro-Union attitude, for a glaring example, resulted in the 1863 formation of present-day West Virginia.

A substantial number of Appalachians and local officials in neighboring East Tennessee counties also rebelled against the Confederacy. Consequently, President Lincoln requested that one of his most trusted generals, Oliver O. Howard (the namesake of Howard University), reward them for their loyalty should anything happen to him. The following article says it all:

Obviously, Tennessee's coalfield residents were not just lukewarm about preserving the Union. More than 30,000 of those southern Appalachians joined the Union Army, which reportedly was the highest geographical per-capita ratio in the nation. In fact, the very pro-Union, coal-bearing county of Scott seceded from Tennessee, a Confederate state, due to slavery and a strong fealty to the American flag.

As a result of General Howard's promise kept, Lincoln Memorial University (LMU) was founded decades later just two miles from the Virginia border in the town of Harrogate, Tennessee. Today, that fast-growing private, faith-based school provides mountain students and young people from around the globe with opportunities to become doctors, lawyers, veterinarians, allied healthcare specialists, business and education leaders, and, very soon, dentists.

A Lee County, Virginia, mountain native and eventual LMU graduate, Autry O.V. "Pete" DeBusk, lived in a dozen or more coal camps and towns as his father built coal tipples throughout the coalfield region. Pete learned how to get along with strangers as he switched schools every few months. He went on to prosper in the medical supplies industry and became the originator of dozens of patents in that field, including the world-famous soft boot cast.

Pete is now the chair of the LMU board. Through his visionary zeal and generosity, this son of the mountains has helped thousands of

Appalachian students receive undergraduate and graduate-level educations they likely could not have accessed without his dedication.

Pete, like many of our Appalachian local leaders, was born of a nurturing culture.

Autry O.V. "Pete" DeBusk

I usually get blank stares from my buddies, or participants in leadership programs I address on occasion, as I count these and other ways that we coalfield Appalachians are far different from the stereotypes others are so apt to inhale and repeat. I am not sure if their stares are due to disbelief, awe, or not fully understanding my mountain dialect, but they are painfully hilarious nonetheless.

But, back to the history-making first and second presidential runs made by our first African-American president. Those two elections supply ample evidence to show that racism here in the Appalachian coalfields is not as pervasive as political pundits like to portray.

For example, in Southwest Virginia the 9th Congressional District (at that time) ran 200 miles from Salem westward to the Cumberland Gap. It is conservative territory no doubt, but the past three pre-Hillary Clinton Democratic presidential candidates, Gore, Kerry, and Obama (all three arguably the most liberal U.S. Senators at the time), each garnered about 39% of the vote.

And let's not forget Doug Wilder's historic 1989 victory as the nation's first African-American governor. He won Virginia's governorship by a razor-thin edge and carried five of the seven coalfield counties by margins from 54-62%! Meanwhile, he barely carried blue-blooded Albemarle County with a tepid 51%. Many political pundits of that time (including the candidate himself) opined that the coalfields supplied him the boost necessary to make history.

Doug Wilder, campaigning in Lee County with a Democrat war horse, Edgar Bacon.

The obvious question then is if we are such racists here in the Appalachian coalfields, how did Barack Obama pull the same percentage of votes in his first run as two of the whitest guys in America?

It is no big surprise that President Obama did very poorly here in his re-election bid because by that time his attitude toward coal, gun rights, and late-term abortions were well known.

And Hillary Clinton did not help her cause when she looked straight into the TV camera and promised to cut out the highest paying blue-collar jobs in the coal region and, at least by implication, averred that coalfield Appalachians were amongst the most deplorable of the deplorables.

Imagine if she had said that reporters and journalists were stale-dated due to the Internet, had run their course, and were no longer needed, thank you very much! I am fairly certain that she would not have garnered their majority support either.

Agree with the coalfield majority's stance on these hot-button issues or not, the 92% White voting bloc in Virginia's Ninth Congressional District gave President Obama his equal share of votes until it became clear how he felt about us "clinging" to firearms, Bibles, the American flag, and life-sustaining jobs. Voting "no" to his second term after these revelations was based mostly upon fact-driven microeconomics and democracy, not racism. And how did Governor Wilder prevail in his historic coalfield campaign if we were, and are, the knuckle-dragging Neanderthals depicted on both coasts?

In other words, our coalfield region had a history of inclusion way before more genteel regions of the nation and Virginia were ordered by courts to do so. Court-ordered public school integration in the coalfields was relatively seamless, while some rabidly racist Virginia jurisdictions further east and north privatized schools in a vain attempt to avoid the law of the land. It took decades in these same radical communities of the state to reach near-full compliance. Even today very worried old-timey liberals opine that our nation's most "progressive" cities and ultra-woke colleges have "back-slid" toward segregation.

These Woke academic leaders apparently have forgotten Martin Luther King's life-and-death struggle to not be judged or segregated by the color of one's skin.

5

EDUCATION AND ATHLETICS

Speaking of schools, the notion that Virginia's coalfield residents are impoverished (mostly true) and therefore deemed to be ignorant (a bald-faced lie) needs to be openly addressed. Virginia's 133 school districts are divided by its department of education into regions numbered one through eight. Region 7 is home to all the coalfield counties and the adjacent mountainous agriculture lands to the east, more commonly referred to as Far Southwest Virginia or the "Great Southwest." (Admittedly, that last moniker may confuse folks; they may end up in Arizona trying to find us.)

Not so long ago while meeting in Richmond with state and college officials about bringing high-tech jobs to our mining region, I was point-blank asked if our students had the DNA "down there" to handle such sophisticated jobs. After spewing a few visceral comments, I calmed down enough to lay stats on them that debunked such bigotry. My counter-stats went something like this: For the past several years, the students of mountainous Region 7 have scored far above the state public school average in their Standards of Learning (SOL) tests in math, science, and reading. More recently, our young brainiacs bested all other regions, including super rich Northern Virginia, in these academic achievements. Not a peep, good or bad, came back at me.

I literally have friends and family members who doubt that our Southwest Virginia kids were number one in the state (pre-COVID) regarding public school academic rankings. That's understandable, many times the victims of denigration and slander start believing the bad things said about them. This lack of self-confidence is generational in poor communities worldwide. Step one to succeed is to get on the positive side of life in order to counter the trolls.

Let's address in more detail the very harmful outsider assumption that coalfield Appalachian children are "dumber than a sack of hammers." (phrase credited to George Clooney in the best movie ever, *Oh Brother, Where Art Thou?*)

Wise County, the second largest coal producer in Virginia, ranked number 4 out of 133 school districts in statewide SOL scores, while super-rich Albemarle County ranked 66th. The state's remaining coalfield counties' pass-rate rankings were as follows: Scott 9th, Tazewell 10th, Russell 13th, Dickenson 16th, and the City of Norton 19th. You get the picture. Only Lee and Buchanan counties lag behind regionally. (*These SOL stats are pre-COVID due to the lack of remote access learning in the outer reaches of rural regions across the nation that grossly skewed prior academic outcomes.*)

How can that truly worst-of-all stereotype of "dumbness" be accurate when Southwest Virginia school systems have consistently been number one or two in SOLs in a state that ranks 4th in the nation for the quality of its public school system?

Much of Appalachia has above average academic successes, while some mountain jurisdictions certainly do not. The failing public school systems nationwide suffer mainly from poor adult supervision and leadership. It is rarely the fault of the children; like young people worldwide they respond to the environment and encouragement fostered by adults.

It is cruel enough to belittle a state, city, county, or town that is perpetually dragging bottom economically; however, it's even worse to ridicule an impoverished region with top scores in one of the nation's upper-tier public school systems. Actually, that is defamation pure and simple.

Commonwealth of Virginia Department of Education
Superintendent's Regions

Let the above chart sink in. The second most impoverished students in the state with the lowest paid teachers and highest ratio of special-needs kids have excelled mightily in STEM studies. Our students have also won multiple state championships in drama, forensics, scholastic bowls, robotics (including 7th in the world for coalfield Dickenson County), and some of our schools have reached extremely elite National Blue Ribbon status. And the list goes on.

Dickenson County's World Class Robotics Team

Just recently, one of the coalfield region's nearest "big" cities, Bristol, Virginia, turned a failing 30% minority elementary school from a 56% SOL pass rate to a 95% score, garnering a national award. One teacher-turned-principal motivated the kids, their community, and her school board to make magic happen, thereby rescuing many children of color from stereotypical assumptions that they cannot keep pace. Imagine the generational fates of the prior students from that school, including White children of poverty that did not have sufficient leaders with vision and tenacity.

This inspirational principal, Faith Mabe, born and raised in the coalfields of Wise County, proved beyond a doubt that adult leadership matters and individuals can make a huge difference for kids. This kind of tremendous turnaround can happen almost anywhere with the right motivators that tap the backing of the community, local officials, and the inspired children that depend upon them to lead and care.

The following full-page ad touting these smart young mountaineers was posted by the author in every major newspaper in Virginia.

FAR SWVA STUDENTS RANK #1
in Standards of Learning Tests in Math, Science, & Reading!

YET OUR SMART, WORKING AGE TALENT DESPERATELY NEED GOOD JOBS

That's right! Far Southwest Virginia public schools are number ONE in the state's Standards of Learning (SOL) tests in math, science, and reading. Three of the eight so-called coalfield school districts (Wise, Scott, and Tazewell counties) are in Virginia's top 10% while three others (Russell and Dickenson counties and the City of Norton) are in the top 15%. These laudable results are achieved by the lowest paid, yet highly effective teachers, as they instruct the second most impoverished students in the Commonwealth.

QUALITY OF LIFE IN FAR SOUTHWEST VIRGINIA

In addition to a strong, trained and trainable workforce other quality of life assets in far Southwest Virginia include the world's highest speed internet; uncrowded primary highways; 1,000 miles of maintained recreational trails; ample fishing, boating, and hunting venues; the Clinch River Valley, which many conservationists deem one of the most biologically diverse native ecosystem in the Northern Hemisphere; wide open spaces with very affordable super-soil farmlands and lush forests; a temperate climate; affordable home and labor costs; low taxes; private, non-profit law, pharmacy, and veterinary graduate schools; the University of Virginia's College at Wise which offers the most affordable public university degree program in the nation; and most important of all, a very friendly, welcoming culture.

BRING YOUR JOBS HERE

We have intelligent, trainable, committed people eager to learn and perform mid-to-high tech jobs that can be filled HERE in satellite centers and co-work spaces. We ask that Virginia's State and Federal agencies transfer unfilled jobs here and that private businesses take advantage of the storehouse of knowledge and capabilities far Southwest Virginia has to offer. We are not asking for a handout. All our youth need is opportunity. We can take care of the rest.

"Companies don't realize what opportunity they are missing. Sure, far Southwest Virginia is a bit far from major economic centers, but we have the access, infrastructure, and workforce they need. The piece we need to market is the culture. A loyal, dedicated, ethical culture is something no amount of money or effort can bring to an area. It's something that is inherent to the indigenous people and SWVA is busting at the seams with it." Power Station Manager, Southwest Virginia Operations

So, don't outsource to foreign lands or pay exorbitant costs for labor in crowded cities only to have expensively-trained employees leave on a whim. Check US out instead!

IT DOESN'T STOP WITH STANDARDS OF LEARNING:

Wise Central High School
- Girls' Basketball Team Wins Five State Titles in Six Seasons
- Back-to-Back State Forensics Titles

Eastside High School
- Drama Team Wins Fifth State Title

Grundy High School
- 22 State Wrestling Titles

Honaker High School
- Top Honors in Scholastic Bowls

Ridgeview High School
- FIRST Robotics State Champion
- Ninth Place at FIRST Robotics World Championship

Saint Paul Elementary School
- National Blue Ribbon Award

Scott County Schools
- State Award for Excellence

Southwest Virginia Community College
- FIRST Robotics Team Earns Spot at World Championship

Wise Central forensics team, back-to-back state champions

COME SEE US!!

If your agency or company wishes to learn more about the opportunities in the mountains of Southwest Virginia, call or email us for a tour. You will visit graduate schools, natural wonders, business and industrial sites, meet innovative leaders, exceptional students, teachers, and professors,

The Ridgeview High School Robotics Team, State Champions, placed 9th out of 64 teams globally

So, what more can and should our young people do to garner respect and coalfield-based job opportunities? We deserve an answer to this bigotry.

Author's Note: For a fascinating account of statewide economic disparities, log onto cardinalnews.org and type in "the numbers we ought to be paying attention to," and review the stat-driven conclusion that **Virginia is the most income-disparate state in the USA** due to hosting the nation's richest communities that border Washington D.C. That stat is then compared to Virginia's rural areas, particularly the coalfields. The article goes on to opine that keeping our smart young people in rural areas is a good start, but we also need to bring back Appalachian business-driven expatriates and recruit newcomers familiar with working online and looking for a better way of life. (Courtesy of Dwayne Yancey, editor of the Cardinal News, cardinalnews.org). Dwayne also raises the issue as to "How the University of Virginia should use its record endowment."

In short, the University of Virginia (UVA) has an endowment of $14.5 BILLION, while its coalfield branch in Wise, Virginia, is struggling mightily to offer new and expanded graduate-level programs that would create very good jobs and other positive opportunities for mountain students.

Just the interest from such a fund would rocket-boost the ability of the University of Virginia's College at Wise (UVAW) to further draw students and faculty not only from Appalachia but around the nation and world. That one move by the mother ship will bring new energy, ideas, and durable prosperity to a chronically poor region. UVAW, in other words, could expand and prosper from UVA's monetary dandruff.

So, it is a constant struggle to whack-a-mole the negative stereotypes that have been hurled our way for decades, even centuries.

For example, until prescription opiate drugs seized Middle America, the flooding of powerful painkillers into poor communities such as Appalachia and inner cities was solely blamed on the victims, not Big Pharma. Now the favored diagnosis and remedies have suddenly switched to counseling and understanding that this is a "public health crisis" mostly caused by greedy drug makers and the few, but deadly, crooked medical professionals in cahoots with them.

When this scourge was raging in poor rural areas and big cities, the solution was jail, prison, and jeering. While it is true that voluntarily taking ill-gotten drugs is ultimately the responsibility of the individual, it is ironic that states are belatedly suing dirty drug companies. Not surprisingly, drug-impacted middle-to-high income communities are no longer advocating the "lock-them-up" solution.

As a side-note, and another point of pride for our mountain region, the U.S. Attorney's office in the Western District of Virginia was the first in the nation to effectively go after drug-pushing Big Pharma. A 2007 case against Purdue Frederick Company and its top executives, prosecuted by Assistant U.S. Attorney Randy Ramseyer, resulted in a $600 million fine and a corporate felony conviction. Talk about being ahead of the curve!

Yet again, this momentous Appalachian precedent was mostly ignored by national leaders and the media. Cynical Appalachians could rationally suspect that these consistent omissions are because we are invisible, therefore disposable. But surely not; no enlightened society would be that mean.

I am hesitant to mention the coalfield region's multiple state championships in sports because way too much emphasis is placed on those non-scholastic accomplishments. Yet sports do demonstrate a general toughness and dedication to excel. Suffice it to say that Buchanan County's seat, Grundy, has won twenty-five high school state champion wrestling trophies as of 2022. The legendary football teams produced by the coal towns of Appalachia, Big Stone Gap, Clintwood, and Richlands also speak for themselves, and that's just the boys! For example, the Wise Central ladies' basketball team won six state titles in the past seven years, and the list goes on.

From Ollan Cassell, who ran track for Appalachia High School and later won a 1964 Olympic gold medal in sprinting; to NFL stars Thomas Jones of Big Stone Gap and Heath Miller of Honaker; and fastball artist Billy Wagner of Tazewell, the Virginia coalfields have accounted themselves well. These irrefutable stats more than show that coalfield residents are a competitive bunch.

Thomas Jones (Stock photo)

Heath Miller (Courtesy of his proud mother)

Billy Wagner (Stock photo)

Ollan Cassell being honored by the Virginia General Assembly in 2020 as the lead sprinter in the 1964 world record USA 4X400m relay team gold medal event. He went on to become the executive director of the U.S. Track and Field organization and a member of the National Track and Field Hall of Fame. (photo by Donnie Ratliff)

Ollan and his teammates celebrate their world record

NFL star Thomas Jones was raised in a coal camp tar-papered house in Appalachia, Virginia, while his mother, Betty, worked in nearby coal mines for twenty years. Her brother, Edd Clark, was a running back for the Appalachia High School Bulldogs in the late 1960s and was known as the "Stonega Stallion," named after a nearby coal camp where she and he were raised.

Edd set the high school state record for total rushing yards, 5908, scored a career 566 points, and ran the most yards rushed in a single game, 449, only to have the latter record surpassed by his nephew, Thomas Jones, at 462 yards. Jones played football only two miles away at Powell Valley High School. When calculating career yardage and scores, one should keep in mind that until the early 1970s there were no state playoffs in Virginia for the smaller schools, where stats can pile up. Edd struggled academically at Purdue and did not penetrate the NFL like his two nephews, Thomas and Julius. Their locally famous uncle, nonetheless, was much of a hero. He drowned in Florida while saving children caught in an ocean undertow. Exhausted, he attempted to save another child and died trying. The Stonega Stallion will never be forgotten in the Virginia coalfields.

Edd Clark

So if our mountain kids are so smart and competitive, why are state and federal agencies and the high-tech private sectors not rushing here to recruit, train, and employ them in place at great savings in salaries and more favorable attrition rates? That is a good question and millions of public dollars have been spent on studying the answer.

Hopefully, the answer has been provided hereinabove, to use a worn-out legal term. Negative stereotypes, slanderous presumptions, a lack of national acceptance and awareness, and toxic sages such as J.D. Vance, hurt our mountain children.

As a result, a majority of our brainiest leave in bunches each month of May, with high school diplomas in hand, to seek careers elsewhere. Once there, they create jobs, enhance their adopted communities, and become productive political and civic leaders in distant places while we suffer from a shortage of all of those qualities and human assets. Many, many of them would stay, or come back after learning their crafts, if we had the appropriate jobs to offer them.

Simply put, a modern society cannot survive—much less prosper—when today's best and brightest talent and tomorrow's potential leaders leave as teenagers. So yes, negative stereotypes hurt in real ways and we mountain people sure could use an Appalachian anti-defamation league. Maybe some young mountain savant will study this writing and lead the charge; otherwise, we are on the bumpy road of no return.

But, some skeptical readers might say, this is all in the past and the friendly culture of the coalfields is no more. Let's review a more recent example that such traits still exist when it comes to welcoming strangers and respecting other ideas and religions.

Buchanan County's Appalachian College of Pharmacy, which I founded, very much needed a pharmaceutics professor so that the school could attain full accreditation. The problem was that the pharmaceutical industry at that time hired every PhD in the field that they could find. We were in trouble. Fortunately, a highly qualified immigrant from Bangladesh responded to our ad. We promptly fired an administrator, also an immigrant, for failing to hire her because of her religion. Upon learning about this despicable slight, she received an appropriate interview and evaluation that I conducted.

Dr. Masuda then became one of our hardest working and most

dedicated employees at the school. She, her husband, and two brilliant daughters were respected and helped by any and all mountain natives they came to know. We found them housing, lean goats, and a mosque, and quickly became their travel guides, friends, and colleagues. In turn, they invited our multi-cultural science faculty and other lucky guests to their home and laid out a feast of curried meats, delicious vegetables, and incredible desserts.

Try being asked to say grace over a meal hosted by a Muslim family whose guests included Jewish professors, Seventh Day Adventists, Hindus, Baptists, agnostics, and atheists!

Trying not to offend anyone, I sputtered like the Rain Man until being rescued by my wife, a seasoned grace whisperer. This is the same Muslim family that graciously forgave me for inadvertently introducing them to pork because I forgot that the Appalachian feast I fed them in return had "fat-back" meat in the pinto beans.

I could not have been prouder when this Muslim wife and husband team interviewed with the *Richmond Times Dispatch*, and declared that of all the places they had lived—including Saudi Arabia, Canada, Texas, Utah, and Florida—they felt most welcomed in the Virginia coalfields. After they eventually moved away to Richmond, I visited them again as newly sworn U.S. citizens. They warmly reiterated their desire to come back "home" to Appalachia. I hope they do.

Proud U.S. Citizens, Shams Rahman and Dr. Quamrun Masuda, presenting a bountiful South Asian meal, topped off with American apple pie.

And speaking of Buchanan County, likely the most maligned Virginia coalfield county due to its remoteness and being squeezed between two other coalfield states, Kentucky and West Virginia, there is a wondrous story of inclusion to tell.

In 1921 a Buchanan County orphan, Sam Hurley, decided to help other at-risk children by founding Mountain Mission School in the town limits of Grundy. Thousands of impoverished (and sometimes abused) mountain kids received housing, education, and inspiration from this faith-based safe place over the decades. As more and more social programs became federally funded in Appalachia, the need for private endemic orphanages waned.

The school had a choice of closing down or reaching out to other desperate children. Hence, the majority of its impoverished students have more recently originated from approximately sixty nations, including many locales in Africa, and Central and South America. A few local children are also enrolled as residents or day students.

In fact, the school has the state's top private and public school diversity rate at 82% students amongst a pre-COVID student body of 260. Its choir is world-renowned, and the college placement rate is routinely over 90%.

Mountain Mission Choir

Mountain Missions School as NACA 2022 National Champions
in Division IV Girls Basketball

Appalachian orphans at Mountain Mission School, 1950s

Sam Hurley at the groundbreaking for Mountain Mission School

Mountain Mission student, a future herpetologist, 1940s

To ensure the 100-year-old school's sustainability, two big-name golf tournaments hosted by a Buchanan County native and former coal operator, Jim McGlothlin, raised more than $70 million. Plus, Mountain Mission graduates who aspire to attend college matriculate at some of the best universities in the nation. They do so debt-free, or near so, because of Jim, his wife Fran, and many other dedicated benefactors.

Like most Appalachians, Jim was taught by his parents, Woodrow and Sally, to help people in need, particularly children and the elderly, and to be gracious to strangers and the people around you, regardless of poverty, creed, or race. This nurturing culture is the very good side of coalfield Appalachia.

6

APPALACHIAN MILITARY PARTICIPATION AND STANDOUTS

I previously noted that Appalachians are patriots "to a fault." This accolade is borne out by the following *Baltimore Sun* article reprinted in memory of the author, Alice Cornett, a prolific and well-respected writer of Appalachia.

The Sgt. York Syndrome
by Alice Cornett
November 11, 1991 | London, Kentucky

London, Kentucky — When U.S. casualty figures in the Persian Gulf War are analyzed, we may learn that this war ended not only the "Vietnam Syndrome," as President Bush proclaimed, but also the so-called "Sergeant York Syndrome," the disproportionate number of casualties among servicemen from Appalachia.

As a percent of its population, the Appalachian region has sustained higher losses in our wars of the past 50 years than has any other section of the country. West Virginia, the only state designated as wholly in Appalachia, had the highest casualty ratio in both World War II and the Vietnam conflict.

In Vietnam, West Virginians died in combat at a rate of 84.1 for every 100,000 of the state's male residents. The national average was 58.9 deaths per 100,000 males.

Parts of 13 other states are classed as Appalachian counties, and these outdistanced the non-Appalachian counties in Vietnam casualties. Kentucky's Appalachian counties averaged 84.2 deaths per 100,000 males; the rest of Kentucky averaged 64.4.

Ohio, generally perceived as a Midwestern state, has a few Appalachian counties along its borders with West Virginia and Kentucky. These averaged 78.4 losses in Vietnam per 100,000 males while for the rest of Ohio, the figure was 59.5.

Theories put forward to explain this startling disparity have focused on the character and the military heritage of residents of Appalachia as well as the region's perennially poor economy. Unshakable patriotism and a willingness to fight for his country have long been attributes of the Southern mountaineer.

That tradition goes back to the Revolutionary War Battle of Kings Mountain where backwoodsmen from western Virginia, the Carolinas, and Georgia sent the British trained Tories packing.

Breathitt County in Eastern Kentucky won distinction during World War I as the only county in America without a single draftee. Its military quota was readily filled by enlistments. Poverty cannot be overlooked, however, as an impetus to military service. With limited access to higher education, and never enough jobs to go around, many Appalachians have found few alternatives to military service. The probability of being killed in war seemed scarcely greater than that of being killed in a coal mine.

In a 1976 *Washington Monthly* article, James Fallows called Vietnam "the class war," pointing out that although Selective Service was in effect, Vietnam was our first war in which all segments of American society did not participate equally. The wealthier and better educated remained in college, sought other legal loopholes to the draft, or left the country. Those who did the fighting, Mr. Fallows wrote, came by and large from the underclasses—Appalachians, Blacks from the inner cities and the South, and Hispanics from the barrios.

While this argument would seem to have validity, it does not account for unequal losses based on a purely geographical standpoint. Statistics make clear that an Appalachian's chance of dying in battle for his country has been significantly greater than that risk has been for other Americans. It appears that certain characteristics—including a particular aptness for combat—have made him a prime target.

"Appalachians make good soldiers, and the Army knows it," said Steven Giles, chief psychologist at the Mountain Home, Tenn., Veterans Administration Medical Center. Dr. Giles, who compiled a study of U.S. war casualties, is credited with coining the term "Sergeant York Syndrome." Sgt. Alvin York was the Tennessee mountain man who single-handedly captured 90 German soldiers in the Argonne in 1918 and received the Medal of Honor. York had been a conscientious objector to the draft, but was persuaded that military service was not incompatible with his beliefs.

Although they serve in all branches of the armed forces, Appalachians are especially valued by the Army. As recruits, they arrive already familiar with the rifle, the infantryman's weapon, and with knowledge of rough terrain. Officers interviewed by Dr. Giles told him that men from Appalachia were preferred for patrols, or to "walk point"—leading the platoon into unknown territory.

Nine percent of U.S. military forces in the Korean War were from areas of Appalachia, but 18 percent of the Medals of Honor awarded in that war went to Appalachians. In Vietnam, they made up 8 percent of our troops and received 13 percent of the Medals of Honor.

In the Persian Gulf War, U.S. fighting tactics changed dramatically. The emphasis shifted from the foot soldier to sophisticated weapons systems delivered by aircraft or launched from remote sites. The new combat style appears to hold a promise that the unequal losses in past conflicts may never be repeated. In fact, our casualties in Desert Storm were so light that, for statistical purposes, they may be inconclusive—and it is too soon to say whether the Sergeant York Syndrome still operates. Perhaps it will not outlast this century, or this generation.

[end of article]

While many, many Appalachian warriors received the Medal of Honor and other citations for valor in combat, two of them stand out. Sergeant Alvin York, mentioned by Cornett, is buried in his coalfield county of Fentress, Tennessee. His faith, grace, combat readiness, skills, and tactics during World War I are well documented and showcased by Hollywood.

Closer to my childhood home, five miles to be exact, a rambunctious young man from Castlewood, Virginia, became the unofficial Sergeant York of World War II.

Junior James Spurrier (born James Ira Spurrier) was a U.S. Army soldier who received the military's two highest decorations for valor, the Medal of Honor and the Distinguished Service Cross. He also received the Croix de Guerre from France and a like medal from Belgium. Overall he received 17 military medals during his WWII stint.

Junior dropped out of Russell County's school system in the sixth grade to help his family during the Great Depression. When his mother died, he joined the Civilian Conservation Corps in West Virginia to send money back home, like many young people did during that time of nationwide poverty. Soon thereafter, Uncle Sam had other plans for these work-hardened young men, so Junior came back home to Virginia and enlisted in the U.S. Army at a Richmond induction center.

He first fought in the Pacific Theater, and after being seriously wounded came back to the states for medical care. When deemed fit to return to service he requested to go back to the battlefield. He was assigned to the 35th Infantry Division and shipped out to Europe after the D-Day invasion.

On September 16, 1944, near Lay-Saint-Christophe, France, Junior personally assaulted a hill where German defenders were dug in and raining hot lead and mortar shells upon the American soldiers below. After his unit took cover, Junior manned an abandoned machine gun and in short order killed over a dozen Nazis and forced the surrender of twenty-two more. Running out of ammo, he, through stealth and determination, circled behind active machine gun nests and hurled hand grenades that sent many more Nazis to Hades, much to the delight of his pinned down buddies. The estimated German fatalities imposed by this single fighter ranged in the dozens. Counting bodies while chasing the "Krauts" was not a priority as U.S. soldiers pressed Hitler's forces out of France and into their native country, for the ultimate coup-de-grace. Obviously Junior favored up close and personal valor.

Then on November 13, 1944, this mountain Rambo singlehandedly attacked dug-in German forces in Achain, France. By that time this very independent 22-year-old scrapper had a reputation amongst his officers and fellow soldiers for deciding on his own how best to annihilate the enemy. While his fellow soldiers waited for the command to attack, Junior slipped around to the rear of the town and started waylaying Germans, alone. A reporter for the American Legion Magazine, who was familiar with Junior, concluded that after swiping a can of peaches from the mess sergeant and feeling very frisky, he jumped the orderly lineup "secretly hoping there were enough Germans in the place to give him a fight."

Hearing the premature noise of machine guns, rifles, grenades and at least one bazooka, the commanding officer, Colonel Roecker, inquired by walkie-talkie what had happened. His combat officer reluctantly speculated that Junior must had been impatient and started the battle without them. The Colonel then gave this epic order: "Attack Achain! Company G from the east and Spurrier from the west!"

The rest of the main unit attacked as directed and was promptly pinned down by blazing machine gun fire. With very little combat help, Spurrier liberated the entire occupied town that day after hours of hide-and-seek tactics. He used a Browning Automatic Rifle, his M1 rifle, a captured bazooka, various pistols, plus American and German hand grenades, all the while under intense fire.

The surviving Nazis who did not flee sought refuge in a barn filled with hay and barrels of fuel. Like any clever country boy would have done, Junior set this very volatile mix on fire! He then captured numerous soldiers as they ran from the inferno. As Hollywood might have scripted, he ended his assault while operating a "borrowed" German motorcycle. As he sped through the corpse-littered village streets, Junior clipped another enemy soldier or two with pistols blazing. During these several hours of combat he killed a German officer and twenty five enlisted soldiers, captured two more officers, and nabbed a dozen more erstwhile Aryan supermen.

His final estimated kill and capture counts of the two battles combined: 40-60 dead and 36 captured Nazis; Hitler, 0.

Junior received the nickname "Task Force Spurrier" from his unit. He earned it.

After returning home he pitched for a minor league baseball team in Galax, Virginia, and decided he was a better soldier than baseball player (with a 1-1 record). He re-enlisted in the Army in 1947 and eventually found himself in Korea.

Due to what we now know as PTSD symptoms, made worse by alcohol, he was routinely disciplined and in 1951 received a general discharge. Back in the States, Junior was easily agitated and got involved in more than one ballroom brawl. I can only imagine what happened when some tanked-up honky-tonk bully challenged Junior to step outside to fight!

After his last brush with the law, Junior stopped drinking and became a radio and TV repairman. This mostly unheralded American hero lived in a Tennessee cabin until his death in 1984. This sad ending takes nothing away from his undaunted courage and love of country. Junior's battlefield exploits were captured by this Army illustration:

Credit: Yank Magazine

A painting of the likeness of Staff Sgt. J. I. "Junior" Spurrier receiving his medal of honor from General Dwight Eisenhower in February of 1945 hangs in the Mercer County's "Those Who Served" War Museum in Princeton, West Virginia.

MEDAL OF HONOR
SSG JUNIOR J. SPURRIER
WORLD WAR II | 13 NOVEMBER 1944

STAFF SGT. JUNIOR J. SPURRIER

Back Home in Coalfield Appalachia

Author's Note: Tax-deductible donations for a long deserved memorial site to honor Junior can be made out to Mountain Heritage, Inc. P.O. 1259, St. Paul, Va, 24283.

PS: By the way, when is a movie about this unsung hero going to be produced? Someone with connections please call Brad Pitt, Clint Eastwood or Rambo. They won't get back to me, must be my dialect.

Shifty Powers

If you have seen the *Band of Brothers* series you will recall Shifty Powers, the coolest sharpshooter in the outfit. He was raised in Clinchco, Virginia, a very small coal town located in Dickenson County. Residing across Hazel Mountain about 25 miles from my boyhood home, he got his nickname for shifty basketball moves.

Like all Appalachian boys of that era, he was taught at a very young age how to effectively use firearms and be stealthy while hunting squirrels, grouse, ground hogs, and such. Larger animals— deer and turkey, for example—were very scarce in the coalfields when WWII broke out. Mountain families struggling to live day to day during the Great Depression cleared out most of the wild game, and only within recent decades have deer, turkey, bear, and bobcats made a big comeback.

Shifty was the man the field commanders called upon when a long shot at a distant Nazi sniper or forward scout was in order. Evidently, he perfected the head-shot-under-pressure and did his part to end the war. Like my WWII dad, he hated Nazis until the day he passed!

Shifty Powers, a true patriot.

7

COAL MINING

Of course, like many communities worldwide, especially where poverty reigns, Appalachia has a dark side and those negative images always seem to "hawg" the headlines. We are easy targets because of rarely fighting back, but that seems to be changing.

Because it would be impolite to not mention our neighboring coalfield states (that also have histories of inclusiveness and Union loyalties) a brief description of those communities, labor union struggles, and feast-or-famine economies is offered up for context.

But first know that most readers of this book will be surprised to learn that many of our fifty states have mined coal at some point in their histories. As mentioned, the first commercially mined coal by Europeans and their descendants occurred near Richmond, Virginia, in 1701. The first Native Americans to use coal are believed to be the Hopi tribe in the 1300s. Even Hawaii had small deposits of the black stuff in collapsed volcanoes that filled with rotted vegetation over the years before forming into peat, then sub-bituminous coal.

The following map sets out the nation's areas of coal deposits ranging from anthracite, bituminous, sub-bituminous, and lignite, listed in order of purity:

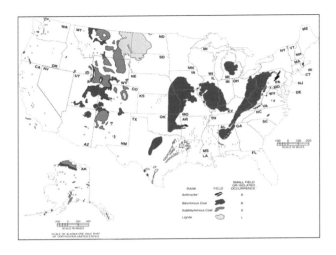

The states of West Virginia, Pennsylvania and Kentucky have always been on the top production list for Appalachian coal, some of the purist in the world. Outside of Appalachia the state of Wyoming currently, by far, produces the most coal of any state in the nation, yet its BTU (British Thermal Unit) quality is far less than the more ancient coal in our mountains.

Ohio, which certainly will be making news during J.D.'s senate race, mined its first coal in 1800, way before most Appalachian venues did so. That state is a powerhouse of coal-fueled electricity and is still sitting on about 5% of the nation's coal reserves.

It will be interesting to follow that state's coalfield support for the young senate candidate after the very negative things he said (not so long ago) about the former president and demeaning Appalachia and her people in his book and movie. His abrupt about-face regarding those topics surely dislodged a hard-to-detect vertebra or two.

Coal production in the Appalachian states has plummeted during the past decades, particularly the past several years. As steam coal demands dry up due to power plants switching to cheap (and less polluting) natural gas and renewable sources, the only secure source of coal jobs emanates from the mining of metallurgical coal used for steel production.

Appalachia still hosts a substantial supply of high-grade "met" coal seams and, unless a substitute for coking coal is developed, the only coal mining jobs in Appalachia will eventually be of that variety.

Metallurgical coal seams, such as the Pocahontas variety, that run through parts of southwest Virginia and southern West Virginia, have a BTU content of 15,000 or so (triple that of Wyoming coal). This Appalachian "rocket fuel coal" burns so clean that it is referred to as "smokeless." Much like anthracite coal located further east in the Appalachians, the purity of coal depends upon geological pressure, the age of the coal's formation, and how the great swamps that produced the peat moss (that turned into coal) were mixed and matched with sand, mud, and trace minerals.

While many coal-mining advocates tend to blame the EPA for coal's decline, there are many factors at play. The EPA, in reality, does not have primary oversight of coal-mining-related environmental issues. Those regulatory enforcements rest on the federal level with the Office of Surface Mining (OSM) and myriad state agencies that have primacy as long as they follow federal guidelines set forth by Congress in what is usually referred to as the Surface Mining Act of 1977.

The overall decline of eastern coal was already in progress when tighter enforcement of existing laws was vigorously applied under the Obama administration. Federal courts also gave opponents of mountaintop removal operations an edge for the first time through stricter interpretations of permanent streams and other hydrological issues. The following map is useful in tracking coal deposits and poverty in Appalachia:

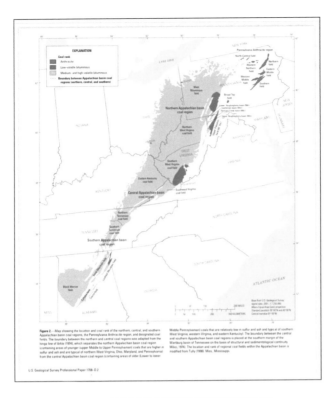

Figure 2.—Map showing the location and coal rank of the northern, central, and southern Appalachian basin coal regions, the Pennsylvania Anthracite region, and designated coal fields. The boundary between the northern and central coal regions was adapted from the Isorup line of Arkle (1974), which separates the northern Appalachian basin coal region (containing areas of younger upper Middle to Upper Pennsylvanian coals that are higher in sulfur and ash and are typical of northern West Virginia, Ohio, Maryland, and Pennsylvania) from the central Appalachian basin coal region (containing areas of older (lower to lower Middle Pennsylvanian coals that are relatively low in sulfur and ash and typical of southern West Virginia, western Virginia, and eastern Kentucky). The boundary between the central and southern Appalachian basin coal regions is placed at the southern margin of the Wartburg basin of Tennessee on the basis of structural and sedimentological continuity (Milici, 1974). The location and rank of regional coal fields within the Appalachian basin is modified from Tully (1996). Milici, Mississippi.

U.S. Geological Survey Professional Paper 1708–D.2

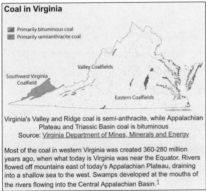

Coal in Virginia

Virginia's Valley and Ridge coal is semi-anthracite, while Appalachian Plateau and Triassic Basin coal is bituminous
Source: Virginia Department of Mines, Minerals and Energy

Most of the coal in western Virginia was created 360-280 million years ago, when what today is Virginia was near the Equator. Rivers flowed off mountains east of today's Appalachian Plateau, draining into a shallow sea to the west. Swamps developed at the mouths of the rivers flowing into the Central Appalachian Basin.[1]

It is easy to conclude when mining joblessness rates are mentioned on TV, or the Internet, that laid-off miners can simply switch to other good-paying middle-class jobs. Not so; such occupations are rarely available in the actual coalfields.

Mining and related occupations were the dominant employers in the region for well over one hundred years. Therefore, other potential industries did not locate in the coalfields because of intermittent labor shortages during coal mining economic booms and potential unionization efforts. Unionization is no longer a factor but good work ethics are alive and well.

Another reason well-meaning investors do not target the actual Appalachian coalfield region proper (where poverty and runaway depopulations are most active) is that many of them are geographically misinformed.

For example, when the word "coalfields" is mentioned in the more prosperous venues in Virginia, it is assumed by many job creators that every county west of Roanoke or Wytheville is in that column. The City of Roanoke is 162 miles east of the town of St. Paul, the nearest gateway to the coalfields that lie west of the Clinch River.

Obviously non-coalfield Appalachia in general and coalfield Appalachia specifically have a geographical communications problem added to a long list of other misconceptions. The best rule of thumb when it comes to Virginia is if you are not west of the Clinch River, you ain't in the coalfields. Following that path westward, one soon arrives in neighboring eastern Kentucky. A huge 10,500 square miles of actual coal counties are ensconced there. It's a geology thing: no coal, no coalfields.

To put a face on unemployed miners, *America Al Jazeera* published a February, 2016, article detailing the number of Black families impacted by out-migration caused by the disappearance of this traditional pathway to the middle class.

Coal mining literally offered people of all walks of life, regardless of high school degrees or race, a fighting chance at the American Dream. That opportunity was especially important to impoverished Black Americans, immigrants, and dirt-poor multi-generational Appalachians. The following statistics in the *Al Jazeera* article starkly sum up a dying middle class in the coalfields:

"In the 1930s, coal employed 55,000 black miners. In 2014, the most recent year for which Bureau of Labor Statistics data are available, only about 2,500 black people worked as coal miners — fewer than 3 percent of the total." (written by Roger May for *Al Jazeera America*)

According to this well-written piece, the average yearly income of a

Black family in 1929 was $420.00, while a Black miner could earn $1,400.00. That upward disparity of higher incomes helps explain the reluctance to leave a place known as home, but there is more to that feeling as set forth by the article's author: "Still, (Black) families who've lived here for generations say they're reluctant to leave. They praise the region's physical beauty, close-knit family life and friendly Southern manners."

Read on to discover more about our coalfield neighbors.

8

WEST VIRGINIA

Far Southwest Virginia's coalfields are not the only defamed and belittled portions of Appalachia. Certainly, the crude jokes and vicious slander thrown at West Virginia give that beautiful state a running start as the most ridiculed in the nation. Just ask Bette Midler how the most rabid elitist city folks feel about these impoverished rural Americans.

The coalfield regions of Alabama, Tennessee, and Maryland produce little, if any, coal nowadays, but a similar stereotype stigma lingers there as well. Eastern Kentucky and western Pennsylvania are still major players in what is left of the active mining sections of those states, and their coalfield residents also receive the same cold shoulder and sharp tongue from non-coal region sophisticates dwelling in flatter, more urban environs.

However, West Virginia, located almost totally in coalfield

Appalachia, receives the brunt of the stereotypical derision spewed out by a hurtful cadre of national media talking heads who seem to only visit there to showcase mine disasters or mock the poverty they find during downturns in coal production.

These writers also routinely deride our unique Appalachian dialect that traces its origins to Old England and ancient Scotland, with some vintage Celtic Irish brogue thrown in for good measure.

My Great-Great-Aunt Iney (Ina) Holbrook carried forward many traits of this fading Old Country speech pattern. To provide a timeline perspective, her father-in-law was a soldier in the Civil War and she lived to be 99, passing away in the 1980s. She used the words "kivver" instead of cover, "hope" in the stead of help, "sarvis" in lieu of service and "stob" instead of stab, along with several other variations of words that I did not ask her to explain out of respect for my elders.

I grew up with these ancient words and realized the uniqueness of them when, in 1970, I attended forest ranger technical school in Lake City, Florida.

Being proud of my mountain heritage, I argued with the dendrology (tree identification) professor that, in fact, what he called a service berry tree was, by god, a "sarvis berry" tree. He was a very kind and forgiving soul so gave me an "A" because I already knew the eastern hardwoods from my hundreds of forays in the Appalachian forests with my dad and his dad. I intensely studied Florida's warmer climate beauties such as live oaks, bald cypress, and multiple pine species.

So it is especially galling to be ridiculed by people who speak colorless English, ignorant of the origins of it all. That is because today's outside pundits rarely spend more than a day in our belittled mountain redoubt, if they visit at all, before pontificating their take on a region that is much more complex than coal and hard times. If only they would dig a little deeper, what a surprise they might discover. For the journalists that do remain objective, we thank them. Laura Vozella of the *Washington Post* is an example of telling the good with the bad by personally digging into the facts on the ground through old school interviewing. Obviously every newspaper article has to have a hook to compete with the ever-shrinking competition, but the worn out hook of mockery is not one we appreciate. No one does, by the way.

Let's look at some indisputable facts about coalfield Appalachian egalitarianism and patriotism. West Virginia is the only state in the nation formed from a Confederate state. These mountain people had the guts and principles to part ways over slavery. That's right; the very state that urban writers love to hate, embraced the Union over the Confederacy in 1862 and risked economic collapse and violent invasions from the motherland for voting to stand with Lincoln.

This was a particularly bold move because when the future West Virginians voted to secede from the Cradle of the Confederacy, Rebel forces were racking up battlefield victories on a regular basis. And, on June 20th of 1863, when the United States officially recognized the new state, the tide-turning Battle of Gettysburg had not yet occurred.

So these very independent and rebellious mountain people were not playing the odds that the North would prevail; rather, the majority of the Appalachians residing there, in true Scots-Irish fashion, decided on their own that enslaving fellow humans was not the way to act, and that being mandated by rich slave owners in flat land Richmond (and thereabouts) to fight for the "cause" was not going to be tolerated.

The following pre-Civil War slave population map of the South clearly shows that the darker, more sinister venues where slavery abounded were not in coalfield Appalachia:

How could this be? How could the most ridiculed area in the United States have such a dignified moral history of inclusion and humanity? The newly minted West Virginians suffered mightily for their decision to secede as poverty flourished, near starvation ensued, and untold killings resulted from neighbor-against-neighbor bush-whackings during, and sometimes after, the war.

Those Civil War-related feuds were written up across the national press as violence perpetrated by barbarians rather than the inevitable consequences of the war, especially given the mixed loyalties that emerged in our mountainous states.

For reference, the overblown Hatfield and McCoy feud gave the media plenty of misleading negative fodder. From 1880 to 1891 a dozen people, including members of both families, were killed. That is an average of just over one fatality per year. It could be argued that more people per annum are killed today for jumping lines at pizza and chicken drive-through joints. History and context escape a large portion of the learned class, it seems.

Another example of mountain egalitarianism is the story of McDowell County in West Virginia, which borders two Virginia coal counties. This county was so inclusive of its very large population of African-Americans (30%) in the early 1900s, and beyond, that it was dubbed by the media as "The Free State of McDowell."

One need only watch the "West Virginia" episode from the *Anthony Bourdain: Parts Unknown* series to see that the influence of early immigrants and Black Americans remains there today. Anthony, much better than any PhD philosopher I have met, captured the true essence of coalfield Appalachia, warts and all. The images of a multi-generational love of "home" and the misty mountains that shroud ever-shrinking communities jump through the screen.

At its peak of coal production, McDowell hosted a population of nearly 100,000, many of whom were multi-racial, multi-national, multi-cultural residents, and the county ranked in the top sector of the richest jurisdictions in the nation. Fast-forward, and the reverse is painfully true: A population decimated by the decline of coal-related jobs is racked with the problems every locale in the world experiences when good incomes are no more and poverty takes hold.

As a result of forces beyond the control of its working class, West

Virginia, which hosts the most Appalachians per capita of any state (nearly 100%), can find no escape from elitist wrath. Had J.D. Vance been the self-appointed sage of West Virginia, instead of his non-Appalachian section of Western Ohio, the boy's head would have exploded. So much to mock, so little time.

However J.D. spins it, affirming stories abound when it comes to the inclusive attitude of West Virginia, especially its southern section which is closely tied culturally and politically to far Southwest Virginia. Let's take a further look:

Minnie Buckingham Harper
by I.D. "Duke" Talbott and Charles Murphy

Minnie Buckingham Harper (May 15, 1886-February 10, 1978) was the first African-American woman to serve as a member of a state legislative body in the United States. She was born in Winfield, Putnam County, later moving to the coalfields of McDowell County. She was appointed by Governor Howard Gore on January 10, 1928, to fill the unexpired term of her husband, E. Howard Harper.

A Republican member of the House of Delegates from McDowell County, Mr. Harper died before completing his term. A homemaker and a resident of Keystone, Mrs. Harper received the unanimous recommendation of the McDowell County Republican Executive Committee to fill her husband's position.

Her appointment reflected both the growing role of women in American politics and the maturation of an African-American political coalition in southern West Virginia which, by the 1920s, had become an important part of the party structure of the state.

Harper served less than a term in the House of Delegates, declining to run for the office in the next election. She later married John B. Patterson, a miner, and lived with him in Northfork until his 1956 death. She returned to Winfield, where she died.

[end of article]

McDowell County made state history once again when the voters there elected by ballot an African-American woman to represent them longer than any legislator of that time. Elizabeth Simpson Drewry served from 1951 until she retired in 1966. She was a teacher, member of the governing board of the local American Red Cross, and branch vice president of the National Association of Colored Women.

She received coal miner support by disclosing an attempted coal company bribe and led the way for women to serve on juries, promoted civil rights, championed social justice, and passed health reform measures. Delegate Drewry and other West Virginia leaders promoted progressive agendas before they were cool.

It would be more than 20 years, however, before another African-American woman walked the halls of West Virginia's Legislature. During the elections of 1950, voters in McDowell County elected Elizabeth Simpson Drewry to the House of Delegates, making her the first African-American woman elected to the Legislature. She was extremely active in her role as delegate and a strong supporter of health care reform, teachers and workers.

During her tenure, she is credited with introducing several major bills, including a bill to provide compensation to the victims of silicosis, more commonly known as "black lung disease," as well as the legislation that led to the 1956 constitutional amendment allowing women to serve on juries. She retired from legislative 964, having served longer in McDowell representative at

Delegate Elizabeth Simpson Drewry

This photograph of the Matewan Dry Cleaners is displayed in the Matewan Railroad Depot Replica and depicts John and Mary Brown

(center and right) along with employee "Dad" Caples. This Mingo County business opened in 1910 as the state's first Black-owned dry cleaning service deep, deep into the southern West Virginia coalfields. The Browns retired in 1963 after fifty-two years in business where they were community leaders respected by all that knew them.

In 1918, three Black men were elected to the West Virginia state legislature: Charleston attorney T. G. Nutter; Keystone attorney Harry J. Capehart; and coal miner John V. Coleman of Fayette County.

By 1930, African-Americans initiated and promoted two state colleges, West Virginia State and Bluefield State; a tuberculosis sanitarium; homes for the deaf, blind, aged, and infirm; schools for delinquent youth; a Bureau of Negro Welfare and Statistics; and an expanding number of public elementary, junior high, and high schools.

Few people outside of West Virginia are aware that the second largest ethnic presence in the state (particularly the northern section) is made up of descendants of immigrants from Italy and Sicily. On a less positive note, the fascinating inscription and photo below recount the days of an Italian underground extortion group known as the "Black Hand." The syndicate initially preyed upon Italian merchants and later attempted to extort native business owners and coal miners, which did not work out so well.

"Members of Black Hand Arrested at Fairmont, W.Va."

The more positive note is that the huge majority of immigrants in the Appalachian coalfields worked hard, raised families that went on to work just as vigorously, and made the coalfields hum with life, diversity, and vitality. Add this mix of diverse cultures and passionate beliefs with the native coal miners who were constantly struggling to be protected at work and you can then, at least partly, understand the labor strikes and mining wars that followed.

The nation's largest and most infamous union uprising is known as the Battle of Blair Mountain. Waged in Logan County, West Virginia, it is noted as the nation's largest domestic uprising since the Civil War. For five days in August of 1921, thousands of armed coal miners, many of them veterans of World War I, marched several miles to take on a very corrupt political system that had stymied work safety laws and union efforts for decades.

A previous showdown between the union-supporting Matewan chief of police, Sid Hatfield, versus hired company gunmen resulted in three town residents killed and seven well-armed company-paid Baldwin Felts detectives fatally shot. Better known at the time as "company thugs," these men had just evicted at gunpoint union-supporting miners and their families from company housing. Anticipating swift retaliation they tried to leave town by train, posthaste. They didn't make it. In return, coal companies and the armed personnel they hired resumed even more forceful evictions. When the displaced miners and their families relocated into tent colonies, those were also torn down by the state police.

Chief Hatfield and his friend, Ed Chambers, were later assassinated in McDowell County when Baldwin-Felts gunmen shot the unarmed men as they walked up the courthouse steps with their wives. This ambush provoked what would literally be called a war because it ultimately involved 13,000 miners, 2,000 coal company mercenaries, and the U.S. Army.

Before Army officers finally convinced the miners and fellow veterans to stand down, the workers-turned-guerilla-resistance were allegedly attacked by company-hired private aircraft using a combination of poison gas and explosive bombs left over from the war. Army bombers allegedly provided surveillance according to witnesses.

Even the miners' union and its most ardent supporter, Mother

Jones, tried to quell this growing insurrection in an effort to avoid more bloodshed, but to no avail. During the aftermath of the battle, hundreds of strikers and their leaders were tried on multiple criminal counts. Most of them were acquitted by juries of their peers; largely families of blue-collar workers struggling to survive in a deadly occupation controlled by many corrupt politicians.

In a way, the coal miners of West Virginia, many of whom were and are staunchly pro-American war veterans, literally revolted against a stifling and crooked political system, a cabal that led to the most unregulated and dangerous industry in America at the time.

These working mountain men were not radical idealistic revolutionaries or self-appointed militias rioting to invoke their image of Utopia by overthrowing the nation's government. Instead, they were salt-of-the-earth manual laborers who fueled America's world achievements, including the victorious ending of a recent world war, not knowing that their sons would soon enough face the very same enemy. Coal was so important to both wars that miners could apply for deferrals from military services upon a showing of essential mining skills. Many miners chose the military because of their patriotism and some, I have been told, went to war to avoid the dangers of mining. That says a lot.

Nonetheless, what the miners did at Blair Mountain was obviously violent lawlessness, and what they and their families endured back then was soulless. Neither side should have ever reached that point.

That Appalachian coal miners, past and present, are now tagged as losers and deplorables is very insulting. They paved the way with their dead and broken bodies for millions of blue-collar workers in the nation to be safer at work and command decent wages.

Like participants in many well-meaning movements addressed later in this chapter, some union members abused the hard-fought rights their predecessors died to achieve. Objectivity requires telling both sides of the story of coal, but empathy should be fairly balanced for working people, at least in the world I grew up in.

9

EASTERN KENTUCKY

Teenage boys coming out to the sun.

Eastern Kentucky, just like Southern West Virginia and the far southwestern section of Virginia, has been particularly hard hit by the decline of coal-related jobs. When the raw numbers of coal miners being laid off are announced, readers outside the region are likely not impressed by the stats they see.

But those numbers do not reflect the ripple effect of secondary jobs lost. Those positions include truckers, metal fabricators, equipment suppliers, mechanics, tire sales, garage services, and the list goes on. As a result, working-age couples and their children leave these impacted communities in droves.

Consequently, the ratio of higher-wage earners compared to subsistence income recipients are skewed as the consumer power of the population plummets. Thereafter, a domino effect rears its ugly head as the jolt is felt by all providers of goods and services including restaurants, banks, car dealers, and even schools and hospitals; next in line, town and county tax bases melt. Literally, losing just a few good-paying jobs in sparsely populated communities will negatively impact multiple related occupations. Losing hundreds of good paying jobs over a short span of time in any rural community is devastating.

As expected, the Civil War influenced commerce in each eastern state. Kentucky tried to stay neutral during the Civil War, a war that had economic and political impacts in the South for decades to come. Keep in mind that the hot part of the war was over in 1865, but the slow economic recovery in war-torn states lasted until at least the early 1900s. However, commercial mining in the coal-bearing sections of Appalachia caused a big leap in prosperity, regardless of Civil War winners and losers. Even the panhandle of Maryland got into the game.

The overwhelming demand for quality coal during the Industrial Revolution and two world wars allowed the conquered South to diversify its economy from mostly agrarian to a mix of mineral extraction, logging, and related services. The coalfields of the south, for several decades, were the leading revenue sources of many of the coal-producing states. Black and White sharecroppers from the South and immigrants from western and eastern European flooded into the rags-to-riches coalfields. Mining lifted the Appalachian economic boat quickly and in tandem, north to south.

Kentucky did not join the Confederacy due to a deep split in loyalties amongst its residents, particularly in the state's eastern Appalachian coal counties where opposition to slavery was the most prevalent (note the pattern here).

That state's neutrality persisted until a Rebel force tried to take over the government and claim it as part of the Confederacy. No longer neutral, Kentucky's once-uncommitted legislature requested

Union protection and got it. That decision helped the Bluegrass State avoid most of the draconian political and economic restrictions post-war Confederate states worked under for years. This safety net helped Appalachian Kentucky dodge most of the politically driven economic fallout of the war. Thus, Eastern Kentucky's coalfield counties, some of which border Virginia coal counties, also have a history of immigrant and southern Black migrations.

While the West Virginia, Virginia, and Tennessee coalfields were earlier in large commercial coal mining development, Kentucky did, in 1900, join the rush. This delay was partly due to the very expensive process of bringing standard-gauge railroad tracks into the more remote hills.

Coal, being much heavier than agricultural products and timber, required stouter tracks, ties, ballast, and trestles; along with bigger reinforced coal cars and locomotives. Soon thereafter, that coal-rich state caught the wave of labor influx from around the globe. As a direct result, the Appalachian coal-section dwellers in these four states share a much different outlook on domestic life than the surrounding residents of non-coal areas.

Eastern Kentucky has many historical stories of "firsts" in the coal-fields and our nation; a relatively recent example involves the nation's first women coal miners.

In 1974, two ladies from Jenkins, Kentucky, broke that century-old barrier. They resided in Letcher County, Kentucky, which borders Wise County, Virginia. When asked why they sought such a hazardous job, the reply was brutally honest: the money. Laboring at less-productive occupations did not pay the bills, and one of the newly-minted miners was a single mother who entered the deep mines to help her eldest child attend college. They were also the first female members of the United Mine Workers of America, so the news spread fast, with mixed reactions.

Ultimately, this bold move by these two pioneers was mostly celebrated, and several women sought similar positions in the coalfields of Appalachia. As layoffs mounted in ensuing years, the miners with the least experience usually went home first; therefore, very few women are now employed within the mines.

This test of coalfield acceptance of women miners (literally in a man's world) came out as a net positive for the women's movement. To go where no females had ever gone before, and receive equal pay for equal work, was no small feat given that many sophisticated job markets in America today have not yet reached that inspirational goal.

So, Diana Baldwin and Anita Cherry may never make the cut for the top feminist leaders in American history, but at that time they sure did take on one of the dirtiest, most dangerous work in the nation to support their families. Or perhaps had they been residents of another geographical region of the country, where trends are set and such barrier-busting is more celebrated by the media, they would have been widely and ceremoniously recognized. Instead, they were generally viewed locally as plain-spoken, strong mountain women.

HARD WORKING COAL MINERS 1989. Courtesy of Earl Dotter. https://earldotter.com/

Sadly, women miners are not immune to the hazards of coal mining. The stock photo above memorializes Mary K. Counts, a Dickenson County, Virginia native daughter who died in June of 1983 due to a methane gas explosion, along with six male co-workers.

Author's Note: The first woman miner in the nation to lose her life to mining was Marilyn McCuster of Pennsylvania in October of 1979.

The conclusion of an article written about Eastern Kentucky by Heidi-Taylor Caudill and Whitney Hays for the University of Kentucky's Special Collections series describes the current movement to tell the other side of coalfield Appalachia and its inhabitants. While indeed imperfect, the citizens of coalfield Appalachia have for too long been stereotyped as hapless, pathetic figures:

"Stereotypes about Appalachia continue to persist in popular culture, spread largely through the media and entertainment industry. Just as the writings of William Goodell Frost and John Fox, Jr. were published to inform and amuse the American public at the turn of the 20th century, much of today's media about Appalachia exploits the region for attention and money. This treatment has consequences beyond humiliation. As Katherine Ledford, Dwight Billings, and Gurney Norman write in the introduction to *Back Talk from Appalachia: Confronting Stereotypes*, "the "idea of Appalachia" … not only masks the exploitation of land and people in the region, but it obscures the diversity of conditions, relationships, and cultures within Appalachian society itself – diversity of race, gender, and class as well as diversity in religion, education, and history."

Appalachian scholars and activists are now pushing back against the stereotypes and refusing to accept their continuation into the future. Many artists, writers, and musicians in Kentucky have challenged the idea that Appalachia is a homogeneous region with one race, one ethnicity, and one culture. The Affrilachian Poets are one notable example. Kentucky's Poet Laureate Frank X Walker, a founding member of the group and University of Kentucky assistant professor of English, invented the terms "Affrilachia" and "Affrilachian" to demonstrate the role of African-Americans in Appalachian history and culture. According to the group's website, "since 1991, the Affrilachian Poets have been writing together, defying the persistent stereotype of a racially homogenized rural region." Another example is Appalatin, whose sound combines Appalachian folk and Latin music. These individuals and others counter the idea that immigrants and minorities in Appalachian culture have been silenced by the stereotypes.

There is still much work to be done in documenting the multi-cultural history of the Appalachian region and redefining the identity of Appalachians. With further research and increased awareness of the various groups who have lived in Appalachia, perhaps the stereotypes that have plagued the region for the past 100 years will finally disappear into the history books."

[end of article]

An African-American coal community in Eastern Kentucky, 1950s.

10

EASTERN TENNESSEE

Tennessee is rarely mentioned as a coal mining state, but the eastern portion had its heyday for sure and the map below shows the large area of the state involved in the industry:

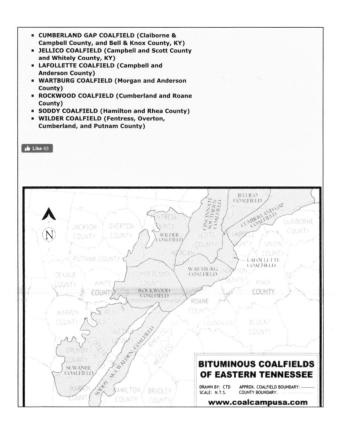

Above and next image: Coalcampusa.com

The following hand-written letter was written by a miner who knew he was dying by suffocation after a methane gas explosion occurred at the Fraterville mine in 1902. The carelessness of the coal company killed 216 miners:

> Ellen, darling, goodbye for us
> both. Elbert said the Lord has save
> him. We are all praying for air to
> support us, but it is getting so
> bad without any air.
> Ellen I want you to live right and
> come to heaven. Raise the childre
> the best you can. Oh how I wish to
> with you, goodbye. Bury me and Elber
> in the same grave by little Eddy. Godb
> Ellen, goodbye Lily, goodbye Jemmie g
> Horace. Is 25 minutes after two.
> There is a few of us alive yet
>   Jatee and Elbert
>   Oh God for one more breath
> Ellen remember me as long as
>   you like. Goodbye darling

Early on, the coalfields of Tennessee and the rest of the Appalachian coalfields were plagued by union and coal company disputes. One such conflict occurred in 1891 when members of the Knights of Labor (a regional coal miners' union) clashed with Tennessee Coal Mining Company personnel and the state over that company's use of "leased" convicts from state prisons.

As a result, the state militia was sent in by the governor to subdue the miners. This ill-advised tactic led to 27 deaths, including several militiamen. The rioting miners sustained hundreds of arrests over a several-months struggle. The illustration below shows the miners firing on state soldiers at Fort Anderson, a makeshift defense garrison:

The miners succeeded in freeing hundreds of convicts, many of whom were Black and virtually enslaved. These southern coalfield mountaineers didn't lynch them, didn't shoot them; instead, they were freed because these so-called replacement workers had no choice in their alleged acts of "stealing jobs." Not being in a position to say no is a big "fair is fair" deal in the mountains.

The Republican Party of Tennessee used this quasi-slavery issue to abolish the convict leasing system. This union-busting maneuver was also prevalent in many other states at that time.

11

THE UNITED MINE WORKERS OF AMERICA

These types of labor violence permeated the Appalachian coalfields as aggrieved miners took great umbrage that safety was an afterthought and that job security was non-existent. These conditions improved after the United Mine Workers of America (UMWA) teamed up with other labor organizations to demand that states and the federal government take action. This standoff went on for more than a century, and today the union is struggling to survive while still pushing for pension and healthcare protection, plus pro-labor legislation.

One of the causes of the union's steady decline of political power and influence emanated from "wildcat strikes," so named because employees would sometimes leave the workplace without UMWA authorization. The only requirement for such a walk-off to occur was the demand of one or more individual miners. Many times these non-sanctioned strikes would shut down all of the coal production for that particular company.

Occasionally these AWOL actions spread to other coal companies that had no hand in whatever the original grievance was about, thereby causing substantial economic losses and breaches of contract with coal-hungry industrial customers, including power plants and steel mills. At times, when asked, the instigators of the strike would not, or could not, clearly state a valid grievance as union leaders attempted to get them back to work to avoid violations of the UMWA's contract with the Bituminous Coal Operators Association (BCOA).

When UMWA members took on the mantra "all for one and one for all" well over a century ago, they literally meant it. The more seasoned coal miners of that era, who had lived through the Great Depression, a devastating world war, and multiple coal strikes, were legitimately worried that such rash walkouts would have permanent and devastating consequences.

My dad Arthur Kilgore, his rowdy brother Harmon, and their workaholic cousin Clinton, many times would report to work at the Moss 2 Clinchfield Coal Company mines just to turn around and come back home because one, usually younger, miner decided he didn't want to work that night. Their late-night-early-morning work period was locally known as the "hoot owl shift," and so it was particularly frustrating to drive back home at 1:00 a.m., empty handed with nowhere to go and nothing constructive to do.

Instead of calling in sick, the disgruntled employee, or employees, would cause their union brothers (and sisters) and the company to lose millions in wages and profits. The elder miners' fear of retaliation against unjustified walkouts became a reality when in 1989 the union's last "big strike" was a do-or-die event for all parties. In a way, it seemed that the Pittston Coal Company drew the short straw amongst unionized coal companies to have a showdown with the UMWA. The company's goal was to either sink or swim, economically speaking. The Pittston coal strike brought the wildcat problem and other festering issues to a head in the coalfields of Virginia, with nationwide labor ramifications.

Wildcatting was only part of the dispute, however, as coal companies realized that pension funds and healthcare costs were mounting and that every bad business decision they made put them deeper in hock. Neither side "won," as Pittston eventually sold its properties and liabilities to non-union companies, most of which eventually went bankrupt.

By that time, many non-union operations were led by a new generation of less confrontational and more cerebral owners who took safety more seriously and paid their miners the same, if not more, than the union scale. All of these factors, plus the increase in automation and a steady drop in demand for coal, leaves the UMWA of today with relatively few members who are actively mining coal. Nonetheless, the United Mine Workers of America's legacy will always be strongly tied to coal and Appalachia.

As I mentioned in my challenge to J.D. at the beginning of this book, my law firm represented almost every union miner and their supporters arrested during the Pittston strike. This protest movement (that started out peacefully, as most often do) generated thousands of court cases, most of which were non-violent misdemeanors. The most serious charges made up about 10% of those cases due to violent and non-violent felony charges.

Although that year-plus long struggle deserves a book of its own regarding its judicial aspects, it is only fair to point out that the UMWA, for the first time that I know of in its history, allowed its members to work without a contract in a vain attempt to avoid a strike.

Pittston, which had withdrawn from the BCOA shortly prior to its decision to go non-union, made no concessions and ultimately took away health coverage support for retirees and demanded mandatory overtime and working on Sundays. It seemed, at least to mining families, that the company took these unprecedented measures just to provoke a strike.

When company support for "widows and orphans" funds was suspended during the fourteen months of working without a contract, the 1,800 Pittston miners were finally authorized by their union to strike. Soon thereafter, 30,000 of the union's nationwide 80,000 active members walked off the job in support of the Virginia miners who were being used as a test to see if the fabled UMWA could finally be minimized, or outright destroyed.

Three lawyer associates, multiple legal assistants, our office manager (my big sister Jean), and I worked around the clock to keep up with the resulting flood of state court labor-related criminal proceedings in eight counties, and numerous related hearings in federal court.

Huge rallies of miners and their supporters generated large donations in support for the UMWA strike fund managed by a non-profit entity. Whenever a "scab" coal mine or preparation plant was designated to be shut down, hundreds, and sometimes thousands, of miners and supporters would block the entrances to the selected facilities.

Some highlights are worth mentioning since I lived this strike well after it ended because our pending court cases still went forward to conclusion. In what may be a national record, my associate, Scott Mullins, and I caused 428 misdemeanor cases to be dismissed after a one-hour hearing. Our clients and supporters packed the court room and hallways of the Russell County, Virginia, courthouse and the milling and passionate defendants not able to find room inside stretched up and down the steep back street. Everyone except the lawyers (I actually thought about it) wore camouflaged tee shirts adorned with strike emblems and epitaphs, some of which were salty for that era.

These particular defendants had participated in a sit-down (and lay-down) strike at the entrance of a huge coal preparation facility called Moss 3 Prep Plant. When built in the 1950s, this technical wonder was the largest coal processing entity in the world.

The Virginia State Police brought in dozens of extra officers to carry out the various court orders mandating that the strikers obey the laws of Virginia and orders of the courts. On this special sit-in day, the state police, the majority of whom treated the strikers and sympathizers with respect, had to carry 428 men and women, large and small, onto buses to have them processed several miles away at a youth detention center in the same county.

Unfortunately for the special prosecutor, the officers who saw the protestors block the entrances were busy loading them onto the buses while other officers at the distant detention center formally placed them under arrest.

Under Virginia law, misdemeanor convictions require that the complaining witness have direct knowledge of the offense, usually by personally seeing the infraction occur, although other methods are allowed, including confessions of course. What is not allowed is for the officer who saw the incident hand over the alleged perpetrator to an arresting officer who did not witness the infraction. As for confessions, not one of our 1,400 or so clients (many had multiple charges) ever talked with state or federal authorities, much less confess. This may also be a national record for non-squealing.

We suggested to the judge that if the special prosecutor, a fine lawyer who was in the U.S. Marine Reserves, agreed with our logic he could put on his best case, and if he lost that argument all 428 cases would be dismissed. Conversely, if he prevailed, all of our clients would be found guilty without further hearings if the judge so ruled. Otherwise, we would have tried the cases one at a time which would have taken several weeks, if not months. Despite the various ethical and technical issues this proposal created, we were fairly sure we would prevail.

The prosecutor readily agreed, and when we cross-examined the token arresting officer and asked him if he saw the token defendant break the law, he had to admit that he was nowhere near the scene of the alleged crime.

Bang!

All of the cases were summarily dismissed and the word spread quickly up and down the hallways and out into the back street. Yelling and whooping ensued as we left the courtroom; back slapping, congratulatory hooting, and macho compliments came from every direction, not exactly what trial lawyers are used to encountering.

To our chagrin, the special prosecutor endured some very graphic suggestions, some of which were anatomically impossible to execute, as he tried to walk through the gauntlet of revved-up miners and supporters lining the hallways and back street, where he had unwittingly parked his car.

I went back to rescue Bob and walked him to his car. Whenever some of my clients would loudly protest that I was "on the other side," I would mention that the prosecutor was a U.S. Marine and Vietnam War vet. The crowd parted like the Red Sea and many of them, especially the war veterans, shook Bob's hand on his slow way out.

Virginia state police arresting coal miners who were blocking a
road to a coal preparation plant.

Gail Gentry, Wise, Virginia, a victim of a coal mining accident.

Prayer at a Russell County UMWA rally

Women miners and supporters during a "sit down" strike, similar to earlier civil
rights movements.

I HAD a few close calls of being arrested myself, which would have been a cred builder among my clients but not so much with the Virginia State Bar.

A local prosecutor was leasing coal rights from Pittston for himself and other investors to mine. It took little effort to convince the court that he had an obvious conflict of interest. His successor was creative, to say the least.

Soon thereafter, I was in the same circuit court awaiting the "true bills" (indictments) issued by the grand jury against several of my clients. The judge solemnly read off the true bills against the suspects who were indicted to stand trial. He then looked at me with a sly grin as he read the last one: "Not a true bill for Frank Kilgore." I did not realize that I was on the menu.

I was a little stunned, and somewhat disgruntled, that the substitute prosecutor thought I needed to be jailed for performing my mandatory duty of informing my clients about the Fifth Amendment of the United States Constitution. But my newly indicted clients thought it was very cool that I was unknowingly before the same grand jury as them and had the skills to avoid their fate. I mentioned that jury nullification was much involved, but they were not having any of that excuse.

I should have basked in the moment, not play it down. I guess I was being too demure as I imagined being led out of the courtroom in cuffs while my fellow lawyers made bets on my fate.

The second time I thought I might be arrested was when a UMWA strike coordinator called with a hypothetical question, or so he claimed. He asked that if, hypothetically, a union wanted to take over, for instance, a soup factory in protest of the company's bad treatment of its employees, what would be the best way to avoid as many criminal charges as possible for doing so?

Still thinking he was joking, I went along with the "what-if" discussion and asked him if the company was publicly traded on the stock exchange and he said yes, hypothetically. So I opined that the union members wanting to take over the soup plant should buy ten shares each of the company stock, storm in and declare a minority stock holders' meeting, and then invite the soup company officers and other stockholders to participate. I promptly forgot the silly conversation; he did not.

Two weeks later, ninety-nine of my clients, all wearing camouflaged clothes and sporting backpacks filled with food, water, and underwear (and possibly Jack Daniels), with the Stars and Stripes waving, rushed the coal company's largest coal preparation plant. This headlong entourage of shouting miners ran off the replacement workers and company security guards in one fell swoop. Each one of the invaders had exactly ten shares of Pittston stock in their pockets.

This takeover made international news and sure enough, the newly minted minority stockholders called a corporate meeting to be conducted at the prep plant. The technical problem was that no outsider stockholder or company official could attend because thousands of striking miners from across Appalachia and their nationwide supporters had the public road blocked for days. After a week or so, I was directed by a federal judge and the UMWA vice-president to go retrieve my clients from the occupied prep plant. The point had been made.

I cannot fathom the number of charges that would have been placed against me, including accessory before, during, and after the fact, if the union coordinator had not explained the actual circumstances to the media. Thankfully, he also disclosed to the authorities that he checked with a lawyer first, without mentioning my name, but that he had made a joke of his hypothetical and then he and the lawyer laughed it off. I was not laughing the day of the takeover.

Below are a few of my prep plant buddies, many of whom are Vietnam War vets along with one or two Korean War elders:

Courtesy of Earl Dotter.

At the time of this all-consuming strike, I had no inclination that thirty-three years later I would be promoting the same 1,800 acre parcel for job-creating industrial development. The shuttered prep plant has been removed and 230 acres of prime, ready-to-build, heavy industrial sites are there today, replete with two electrical sources, multiple railroad sidings, ample water, natural gas, and access to top-drawer solar and geothermal sites. We humans rarely get to truly live a full-circle journey such as this.

Another curious strike-related story involved our local circuit court judge who presided over the strike-related injunction cases. Almost all of the resident judges in the Virginia coal region declared a conflict of interest because they were either from extended union families or had long-term relations with union members during their law practices.

The only judge that did not recuse himself was the son of a veteran state legislator who was very defiant at times and one of the most colorful and engaging mountain characters I have ever met. When some union members pressured him to support their cause he refused, citing the illegal activities that were emerging.

His judge son eventually levied $64 million in fines against the union for violating picket line restrictions and other offenses. These fines were later dismissed by the U.S. Supreme Court upon various legal grounds. Had the fines been imposed, the union would have likely bankrupted.

Courtesy of Earl Dotter.

As a direct result of the local judge's rulings, an unprecedented political movement ensued. His dad, a pugnacious lawyer and two-fisted mountaineer in his own right, came up for re-election during the strike. Being a Democrat, his tenth or so re-election was a foregone conclusion as that party, back then, was locally dominated by coal miner families and union members. They routinely voted as a bloc for the party of Franklin Delano Roosevelt (FDR), a "friend of the working man" and literally the savior and fierce promoter of blue-collar jobs during the Great Depression.

Standing Strong for Jobs. Courtesy of Earl Dotter.

As a kid selling anything from newspapers and garden seeds to glittered wall-hanger religious mottos door-to-door, I noticed that almost every coal miner household I visited had these photos on their living room walls: John L. Lewis (the intimidating titan leader of the United Mine Workers during its heyday), FDR, John F. Kennedy, and Jesus.

That was in the days when the Democratic Party owned the loyalty of Appalachia's rank-and-file workers. This was simply the way things worked politically in coalfield Appalachia as this Democrat state legislator, himself a World War II vet, prepared to win reelection unopposed by any challenger on the ballot.

Literally three weeks before the election, Cecil Roberts, the vice-president (now president) of the UMWA, directed a popular union official from the same county as the incumbent to run as a write-in candidate. The designated protest candidate, Jackie Stump, was jailed, along with Cecil, for several days at the beginning of the strike for violating court orders. Jackie received much press coverage for his ensuing prolonged "hunger strike." Jackie, now deceased, was much of a man and we were mystified when he left jail weighing the same, if not more, as the day he was arrested.

In any event, Jackie at first resisted running as a write-in candidate against a local Democrat powerhouse icon. He feared that he would be the laughing stock of the coalfield region after he got thrashed at the polls and argued that such a loss would, in turn, weaken the union's cause. That was a very clever theory and revealed Jackie's hard-learned lessons after years of navigating his way through UMWA bare-knuckled politics.

Vice-President Roberts was unmoved; he marshaled all of the strikers receiving UMWA-funded weekly strike pay of $200 to go door to door throughout the legislative district and inform thousands of voters that Jackie would not be on the ballot but here is "how to write him in."

Union helpers fanned out over every precinct on Election Day to literally show voters how to complete the write-in ballots, which was a much more obscure process in those days than now. That night Jackie was announced the winner by a 2-to-1 margin.

Everyone assumed he would be a labor firebrand as an Independent and rail against the stubborn remnants of the state's legislative Democrat Byrd Machine, which opposed all unions and openly supported segregation not so long prior to this election.

Being smart, Jackie caucused with the Democrats and their huge majority. He immediately sponsored common-sense bills that had a chance of passing to help not only his avid coal mining supporters but the rest of his constituency that also lacked potable water, good roads, and efficient public services. Unfortunately, his predecessor's ongoing successes in those same efforts were soon lost in the passion of a life-and-death strike.

Delegate Jackie Stump with his baby girl in his Virginia General Assembly office

There are two other unlikely election surprises in Virginia during my voting lifetime that compare to Jackie's improbable victory. One is, of course, the prior election of the nation's first Black governor (in the Cradle of the Confederacy, of all places), and a more recent election involving the nation's first openly transgender state legislative candidate. She handily beat what was likely the most anti-LGBTQIA incumbent in the nation. You cannot write a better movie script than that.

Delegate Danica Roem focused on bread-and-butter issues like traffic jams, while her opponent constantly ridiculed gay and transgender Americans as if they would soon be going door to door seeking converts. This attitude by the incumbent reminded me of my mom's observation that when a person is so rabid about the private business of other consenting adults, he or she might just be unwittingly revealing some deep internal struggle by "protesting too much." It happens frequently.

Like any good Hollywood story, these underdogs won and made history. I could go on and on about the Pittston/UMWA battle, but hopefully my law firm's stash of court cases, recollections, and photos from that epic strike will someday be of assistance to a future author.

To be fair, there were coal companies over the decades that strongly supported local civic efforts. They built schools, churches, and hospitals, and provided running water, housing, and entertainment for their employees and families. Miners had to pay for most of the benefits, of course, but the free new schools and churches were invaluable to a very diverse, pro-religion community. Those new schools, along with missionary facilities and faith-based colleges established by Episcopal, Catholic, Methodist, and Baptist organizations, were a lifeline for education in the coalfields.

Moreover, many of the local coal companies went much further than this to provide for their workers and families. These businesses many times included local owners of non-union mining operations from the mountains who, for philanthropic reasons, helped start and fund many civic, educational, and sports endeavors. Obviously this civic-minded attitude also helped motivate their miners to resist unionization efforts.

I know many coal company owners that I tussled with for decades in court, red-hot politics, and occasionally on a hostile personal basis. Over time, some of us came together to help our coalfield region on many levels.

For example, Jim McGlothlin, the founder of United Coal Company out of Buchanan County, Virginia, has poured in, and is still pouring in, millions of dollars into higher education, job creation, and child development programs, along with helping the entire state advance in art, education, and civic outreach. Jim's boyhood friend Clyde Stacy, and Clyde's business partner John Matney, stay busy creating job opportunities in our mountain region as well.

Buchanan County natives, including Jim's little brothers, Tom and Mickey, were in a position to become number one in philanthropy compared to the rest of the Virginia coalfields. This fortuitous generational outcome came about because northern speculators did not swoop into that more remote county and take the huge majority of the coal and gas wealth back home to city shareholders. Standard-gauge railroads in that coal and gas rich county were not available until the 1930s due to its very steep terrain; that delay was crucial in the accumulation of local wealth.

This opportunity allowed the county's budding local entrepreneurs to figure out that landowners in neighboring coal counties had been hoodwinked into selling their precious commodities for as little as fifty cents an acre. Percentage-wise, many landowners in Buchanan kept their coal intact, which later blossomed into the presence of a generous cadre of benefactors.

Another Buchanan County native, Steve Smith, succeeded his dad,

Jack, in the grocery business. That private chain, Food City, now employs 16,000 workers in Southwest Virginia and Northeast Tennessee (and beyond). Steve and his family step up when it comes to helping their coal and non-coal Appalachian service areas during and after natural disasters, supplying local school needs, marketing locally raised meat and vegetables, and bringing tens of thousands of tourists into the area during sponsored NASCAR events.

Maybe there is something in the water there that engenders "helping thy neighbor." (Disclosure: I represented Buchanan County for thirteen years and we got a lot done, including establishing two graduate schools, the beginning of a flood-proof mega mountain-top development site, and making it Virginia's Elk Capital!) The motto there is "whatever it takes."

Despite these individual efforts, the huge loss of good-paying, middle-class, coal-related jobs holds back generations of smart young people from achieving the goal of recovery.

Although generational wealth is rare in the coalfields, the locals who make it big oftentimes exercise their Appalachian-based sense of generosity and community service. Coalfield Appalachia needs many more locally owned businesses to support a sustained comeback. It will happen when investors looking for a very welcoming atmosphere give us a chance.

Another honorable and former coal company owner, Mike Quillen of Gate City, Virginia, serves on college boards and economic development organizations where he supports many civic and community projects. When he received his first $5 million stock dividend from the company he founded, Alpha Natural Resources, Mike gave it to his hundreds of employees. When I asked him why, his answer was simple: "They are the reason I am successful."

That he and I can now be friends collaborating on coalfield goals was certainly a long shot back in the day when I represented landowners against every coal company he ever worked for as CEO. I also represented a local UMWA official, Sam Church (a man among men and at one time the president of the union), who was accused of assaulting Mike on his own company property during the strike.

I have to say as an aside that Sam did not make my job easier when he came to court sporting a homemade camouflaged tee shirt his buddies put together that depicted him literally carrying out the attack in a cartoonish manner. Sam would not change shirts as I requested, but finally consented to wear a work coat over it before the judge and Mike could see it.

One of the best Sam stories I witnessed involved a poker game in his Richmond hotel room. After a 130-year dry spell, Republicans won a majority in the Virginia House of Delegates. The brand-new Republican Speaker of the House and other legislative dignitaries were playing very loose draw poker and stud when I walked in. Sam previously asked me to participate so he could lobby them for a union cause and not be in the awkward position of taking their money the night before a crucial vote.

My role was to play high-risk hands and be the loser of the night. I approached this role with my usual gusto and would not fold, believing that the odds of me winning were very low. Instead, I hit a very lucky streak and our guests were digging into their pockets often, not happy at all. I was sitting beside Sam, and he very keenly whacked my ankle with his booted foot. I changed course and strategically folded as planned and everyone else seemed happy.

The Speaker liked Sam a lot and said to us all that Sam Church would be the first person he would pick to be in a foxhole with him during a raging battle. Another delegate, without looking up from his cards, said, "Mr. Speaker, if you weren't hanging out with Sam you wouldn't find yourself in a damn foxhole to start with, now would you?!" It was a great time.

Sam has since passed on, but for as long there is a UMWA, he will be honored. The following photo is courtesy of Tim C. Cox (tim@timccox.com):

SAM CHURCH   ©Tim C. Cox

As I advance in age and become more nostalgic about and appreciative of purpose-driven lives, I have come to value and respect many, many of these guys, coal company owners and UMWA leaders alike. Sam felt the same way, and together this mix of unlikely allies has gotten good things done for the coalfields in our own way.

But allow me to be blunt; neither we nor our successors can make a dent without lots of help. There are successful women and men throughout Appalachia that work together as best as they can for young people and future generations. But to really make systemic change, state and federal policy makers, corporate America, and the media will need to be fair and open-minded about embedded cultural smears and negative preconceptions. Doing so will allow our kids, grandkids, and great-grandkids to show their stuff.

So, given this long history of racial and ethnic inclusion, the Appalachian soldiers who helped win the Revolutionary War and beyond, and the miners who dug coal and lost countless lives in violent accidents, there is a simple question I pose: Don't we at least deserve the respect of the keyboard warriors and urban political pundits who now revile and defame us? I think so, or I would not have authored this book.

When debates arise about fossil fuels and the jobs that are lost due to the decline of their uses, some critics of coal and natural gas production fail to understand that they can hate the carbon but should at least empathize with the loss of life-sustaining jobs. These middle-class-paying jobs engender self-respect; they also protect against the lonesome and very scary feeling of leaving a generational sense of home behind to start all over again in a foreign environment.

To hate someone's legal pursuit of financial opportunity should not equate to hate of the person. The ramifications are apparent as such elitist attitudes create resentment; furthermore, that resentment felt by millions of rural voters has political consequences which, in turn, cause even further polarization.

In other words, Americans should not literally hate each other over differences of political opinions or the pursuit of legal occupations. It is a recipe for disaster.

Let's be honest. The worldwide green movement is gaining much momentum due to ever-evolving technology, not name-calling. It took a while for our ancestors to accept the horseless carriage, by the way.

I have been threatened and shot at for supporting federal controls of coal strip mining in 1975-77, back when state legislators and statewide office-seekers cared nothing about impacted coalfield residents (except for campaign contributions they received from coal companies). But each law that I supported resulted in more jobs, not fewer. Environmentalists need that pro-jobs kind of attitude today if they truly wish to cool down the rhetoric. Hopefully green organizations will come to care about jobs other than their own. The Nature Conservancy is a good model for this type of collaboration.

So yes, coalfield residents take great umbrage when talking heads with good jobs, and oozing with privilege, declare that the abolition of coal mining is the only answer. Before coal mining is no more, shouldn't the nation's investors and policy makers help create good job opportunities before the majority of able-bodied adults and their children leave for good? That would be much more politically correct than continuing to disenfranchise rural American voters who feel like second-class cousins, compared to suburban and urban dwellers.

Another news alert: rural people get out and vote, particularly in far Southwest Virginia. Just look at Virginia's 2021 gubernatorial race results as a reminder. Rodney King got it right when he asked, "why can't we all just get along?" And that came from a Black man after he was beaten like a rabid dog.

Our country has repeatedly experienced what can happen when whole populations feel disenfranchised. Now, a new president from the anthracite coalfields of Pennsylvania is advocating innovative job creations in the coalfields, one of the hardest hit regions of America.

If successful, these overdue efforts will be compared to his predecessor who promptly tried to defund the Appalachian Regional Commission, a lifeline to the coalfields. This above average federal agency, founded in 1965, has built thousands of miles of primary roads, installed countless water and sewer lines and facilities, updated housing, provided the world's fastest internet services in key mountain communities, provided support for hospitals, clinics, and dental care, and promoted educational programs toward job creation and leadership. The list goes on, and the uncaring effort to kill this program should not be forgotten.

The result of these recent economic incentives and additional support for federal and state agencies to draw good jobs to a region that has been directly hit by local depression will hopefully be successful. Then many goal-oriented expatriates from these mountains will come back "home." The mountains are already experiencing an influx of newcomer talented folks looking for a less stressful life and that trend needs to be facilitated. We are seeing some of that influx due to violent crime and extreme weather disasters throughout the nation.

I may not live to see it, but I look forward to an epiphany among citizens in the disenfranchised rural areas of America that will cause them to politically team up with disenfranchised residents of inner cities and other struggling venues and together vigorously pursue the quest for good jobs, and the prosperity and pride they bring.

The ONLY way to change generational poverty is to establish generational wealth which must include attracting, becoming, and supporting entrepreneurs. Neither major political party would like to see such a movement; they would, begrudgingly, have to switch their divisive tactics from blatant demagoguery to careful listening.

In other words, high-level political leaders are all so happy to stir up trouble among poor Americans by promising the moon and demonizing their fellow Americans of poverty. The reward received by the politicos in this cynical game means that struggling citizens will cancel out each other's votes. It is a racket.

In summary, the coalfields of Appalachia are known and respected by mountain elders and some historians for many of their residents' opposition to slavery and inhumane working conditions. Thousands perished to preserve the Union during the Civil War, and later on, too many died to create another kind of union to make their ultra-dangerous trade much safer for their children and grandchildren.

It is not a far stretch to claim that our Appalachian coal region was literally the **original home of the progressive movement** when that policy meant supporting working men and women and respecting the differences among us. Coalfield Appalachians, for example, supported FDR, John Kennedy, Jay Rockefeller, and many other forward-thinking candidates. West Virginia, for example, literally salvaged Kennedy's campaign during a primary vote that went his way by nearly two to one. Let's see if Bette can belittle that.

John F. Kennedy campaigning in West Virginia. Note the little boy with a toy gun right behind the future president. Back then it was a normal scene but today we are very aware of law-abiding gun owners being tainted by the seedy population of nuts with triggers. Let's work together on addressing that.

Our struggle to gain a decent living in the mountains is an all-hands-on-deck village effort, now that the beast of living-wage jobless-ness reigns. No longer should we be viewed (or view ourselves) as throw-away people, and our landscape considered to be a national sacrifice zone.

So a memo from the "hillbilly firewall" is in order to our fellow Americans living outside of coalfield Appalachia, and the talking heads who negatively assume too much (or too little) about our mountain character. To-wit: look at the race, gender, and labor relations histories of the place you call home and research the comparative academic achievements in your neck of the woods, stand them all up alongside ours, and with all due respect, find another whipping boy.

Until then, kindly send job opportunities to coalfield Appalachia. Our youths will show what they can do with mid-to-high skilled tech tasks and advanced manufacturing. This life-changing gesture we request will not be a handout; it is simply a challenge to re-evaluate preconceived negative attitudes and help those who are willing to help themselves. "Work" in our mountain culture is not yet a dirty four-letter word.

But to be fair to J.D., we do appreciate the big greenhouse he supported in Kentucky. I hope that soon he will realize he can do much, much more if coalfield Appalachia ever makes his "underserved regions" list.

Then, dast I say, he could create even better coalfield jobs in his Appalachian grandma's honor. Otherwise, he and I need to have that debate on the Bill Maher show I envision daily so we can "go at it." Or, if she is not "canceled," Bette Midler can invite us to her ultra-woke show and answer to both of us regarding her extreme hate and disdain for poor White people (including children by the way). We shall see.

One more note is worth repeating; a big chunk of eastern Ohio is in Appalachia and has a history of coal mining and diversity as well, for example: who do you think was the first Black pro baseball player in the history of the nation? If your answer is Jackie Robinson you would be off about 60 years. Moses Fleetwood Walker played for the Toledo Blue Stockings in the year of 1884, while Jackie went pro in 1947.

Native Appalachians Moses Fleetwood Walker (number 6) and his brother Weldy (number 10), the first Black professional baseball players in 1884.

Where was Moses born and raised? You knew it was coalfield Appalachia didn't you? His home coal county is Jefferson, which borders Bette's favorite state: Wild Wonderful West Virginia. Jefferson was the first county in Ohio to commercially mine coal, in 1800 to be exact.

More specifically, Moses was born in Mount Pleasant, Ohio, which played an important role in the Underground Railroad and the anti-slavery movement. Pennsylvanian Quakers helped get that movement started and many coalfield Appalachians embraced the effort. In fact, Moses' father, Mr. Moses Walker, helped numerous slaves find shelter and food during their long journey and some of them settled in and around this welcoming community as a result.

Mr. Walker was of a mixed race as was his wife. The family early on moved to Steubenville, still in coal county Jefferson, and there he started his medical practice. That town and surrounding area became a hub of immigrants from across western and eastern Europe in the mid to late 1800s to the early 1900s. They lived in and around the town along with descendants of slaves. Newly minted Dr. Moses Walker was one of the first, if not the first, Black physicians in Ohio.

It is very obvious that he, his wife and the Walker children found a diverse and nurturing community in the coalfields of Appalachia that gave them freedom of thought, opportunity and hope in a very racist period that haunted most of America, north and south. What was literally impossible to even think of in most regions of America did happen in our relatively open-minded coal country environment.

Dr. Moses Walker's namesake son was considered the best catcher in the league until injuries cut his standing short after 42 well attended games. Baseball star Moses also exceeded the league's batting average and occasionally shed his chest protector and catcher's mitt during a game. He was a tough and resolute man. His brother, Weldy, was the second African American to play pro ball as he helped his sibling make history on the same team.

Moses, unlike some bi-racial athletes of that time, proudly celebrated his African American lineage and fought racism until the day he passed. He was, after all, raised in a coalfield culture where Americans depended upon each other more than most places and that bond resulted in the impossible happening, again and again.

So, I wonder out loud why this Black Appalachian pioneer is little known while Jackie is a household name? Mr. Robinson deserves all of his other accolades of course, except being first. Maybe the deeply engrained bias against Appalachians in general held back the media Wokes of that era? How could the sub-human mountain caricature many of them presumed and promoted jive with what was actually occurring in coalfield Appalachia both north and south? "Let's play it down boys" must have been the sadistic strategy.

This consistent negative stereotyping theme is very obvious, as spelled out in this book, and, as my college English professor once noted, "it is not paranoia if true." I guess we coalfield Appalachians are too subtle to be heard, or just too invisible.

My bet is that J.D. has no clue about this history of rising equality set closer to his actual home. Given his penchant for sudden adaptability we may now see his political ads embracing Moses. Or maybe not, out of fear that his most radical base may find it upsetting. If he decides to ignore this source of coalfield pride it will seem that he's no more a student of Ohio than he is of the Kentucky mountains he visited as a youth.

It will also be interesting during his senate campaign to see how

J.D. pivots away from the damage he caused mountain people and regional pride with his degrading book and the over-the-top insulting movie that emanated from it. All I can think about regarding that disaster of a picture show, which our Mayberry mountain homie, Opie, shamelessly produced, is that Glenn Close must have had a mortgage payment overdue.

Or, if J.D. is too busy flip-flopping to debate with a real mountaineer, maybe we can skip the talk shows and simply sit down and map out how to keep our kids and grandkids in the mountains they love, with a little less poverty on the side please.

12

THE HISTORY CHANNEL INSULTS ALL APPALACHIANS AND THEIR ANCESTORS

The Revolutionary War in the south, and the participation of Appalachian patriots in winning that struggle, has been purposely ignored. In addition to some Native-American tribes siding with the English in Appalachia, there were also fierce battles among Americans in that seven-year war. The Americans loyal to the King were dubbed "Tories" (or Loyalists), and the pro-revolution Americans called themselves Patriots.

As mentioned previously, an October, 1780, seminal battle fought in the extreme northern area of South Carolina, called the Battle of King's Mountain, literally turned the tide of the war for American independence.

England's General Cornwallis and his highly trained army and naval forces headquartered at Charleston were occupying South Carolina, having already subjugated Georgia, and were on the cusp of overtaking North Carolina.

Cornwallis planned to then attack Virginia from the south while other Redcoat forces pushed southward from northern strongholds. English military leaders foresaw no American forces that could stop these steamroller advances after the epic surrender of thousands of Patriot soldiers at Charleston. If the south fell, the war would be practically impossible for the new nation to win. George Washington's goal of freedom was very much in question.

In the autumn of 1780 a Redcoat Major, Patrick Ferguson, made the fatal mistake of sending a threatening message to the hunters, trappers, and Indian fighters that had settled along the southern Appalachian frontiers, including what is now Southwest Virginia. His dire warning was that if they continued to interrupt the English takeover of North Carolina, death and destruction awaited (as displayed by the National Park Service's "Abingdon Muster Grounds" in Washington County, Virginia):

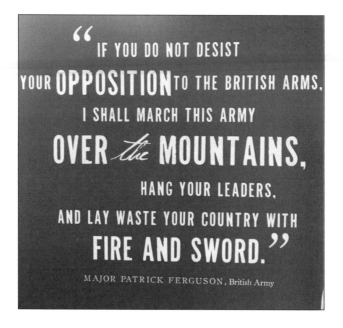

" IF YOU DO NOT DESIST YOUR OPPOSITION TO THE BRITISH ARMS, I SHALL MARCH THIS ARMY OVER the MOUNTAINS, HANG YOUR LEADERS, AND LAY WASTE YOUR COUNTRY WITH FIRE AND SWORD. "

MAJOR PATRICK FERGUSON, British Army

Instead of waiting for Ferguson and his army of Tories to carry out this mission, the mostly Scots-Irish militias from the mountains of Virginia and North Carolina mustered over 1,400 crack-shot fighters to track down and kill the uppity Scottish officer and as many Tories as possible. A contingent of South Carolinians gladly joined the fray in retaliation of Ferguson's role in killing hundreds, if not thousands, of lowland Patriots and their families.

To make things worse for the Tories, an English officer (Tarleton) had, in a prior skirmish, refused to recognize the white flag surrender of defeated Patriots and many of them, including their wounded, were shot or bayoneted. That was not forgotten.

Overmountain Men Looking for a Fight. Artwork by Darris Stanley

Using guerrilla tactics learned the hard way from battle-tested Native-Americans, the French and Indian War, and prior lesser battles against Tories, the men who crossed over the mountains looking for a fight were dubbed the "Overmountain Men."

The opposing army of pro-England Americans was of a similar number, and having the high ground made them very confident as they listened to the crowing of their cocky Scottish military leader. Both armies held back reserves and base-camp attendants so the actual battle numbers were approximately 1,000 men for each side.

Not a big battle in modern terms, but considered sizable in the days of our sparsely populated colonies, especially in the mountains. (Author's note, although roughly 25,000 Patriot soldiers died during the entire seven year war, only 6,500 were killed in actual combat. The rest died of exposure and disease).

The Tories were gathered in a defensive position on top of a low-profile hill, ironically named King's Mountain. Their Major decided that they did not need to entrench to beat a bunch of illiterate back-woodsmen (his very words).

The Patriots used every rock and tree as cover and employed evasive tactics learned from years of rough-terrain battles. They also possessed the world's most accurate rifles, made by Pennsylvania German gunsmiths. These gifted gun makers used the fairly new technology of rifled barrels as opposed to the relatively inaccurate smooth-barreled muskets used by the English forces and Washington's troops.

As it turns out, many of these so-called illiterate backwoodsmen made handsome incomes from fur trading, and therefore could afford the world's best rifles, which were literally their tools of trade and survival.

The Overmountain Men then commenced surrounding and slaughtering hundreds of Tories. Legend has it that Major Ferguson was shot seven times before he became dislodged from his white war horse and fell to the ground, to be finished off. The final lopsided tally is hard to fathom: 290 Tories killed, 163 wounded, and the rest captured, compared to 28 Patriot deaths and 60 wounded.

The battle was difficult to stop even with Tory white flags of surrender popping up. Eventually, the Patriots ceased fire and hastened back to their mountain redoubts. Along the way, some of the Tory prisoners were tried for what we would today call war crimes, and hanged or shot on the spot.

Thomas Jefferson reminisced in his later years that this key battle "was the joyful annunciation of that turn of the tide of success which terminated the revolutionary war, with the seal of our independence." Theodore Roosevelt wrote: "This brilliant victory marked the turning point of the American Revolution." Herbert Hoover went even further as he stood at King's Mountain: "This small band of patriots turned back a dangerous invasion well designed to separate and dismember the united colonies. It was a little army and a little battle but it was of mighty portent. **History has done scant justice to its significance, which should rightly place it beside Lexington, Bunker Hill, Trenton and Yorktown.**"

And get this; Sir Henry Clinton, the British Commander-in-Chief of the Crown's North America war efforts, had this to say about King's Mountain: "an event which was immediately productive of the worst consequences to the King's affairs in South Carolina, and unhappily proved the first link of a Chain of Evils that followed each other in regular succession until they at last ended in the total loss of America."

In less eloquent words, the Overmountain Men overwhelmingly kicked the rears of English forces and caused a ripple effect that won the war.

The battle was the first major Patriot victory to occur after the British invasion of the South. Cornwallis became so paranoid of these and other backwoods killers that he temporarily fortified himself and other military brass against a possible attack on Charleston. One could say that the Overmountain Men were comparable to the Navy Seals of today, given their toughness and deadly fighting skills.

Author's Note: Like most humans, Major Ferguson was not all bad. In 1777, while serving as a young British captain in Pennsylvania, Ferguson—a storied marksman—spied an American officer on horseback with few Patriots in sight. Ferguson aimed his rifle, which he had designed, at the stoic officer who simply glanced at him and slowly moved on. The Scotsman decided not to shoot the American officer in the back. "I could have lodged half a dozen balls in or about him, before he was out of my reach," Ferguson recalled, "but it was not pleasant to fire at the back of an unoffending individual, who was acquitting himself very coolly of his duty—so I let him alone." Afterwards he learned that the individual was likely George Washington, the future first President of the United States.

Don Troiani's description - "Colonel Cleveland's War Prize Oct. 7, 1780." Col. Benjamin Cleveland returning to Wilkesboro on Patrick Ferguson's white horse after his horse, Roebuck, and Ferguson were killed. The patriots took home drums, weapons and clothes. The other colonels awarded Cleveland with Ferguson's white horse, which he rode home. Many consider this the greatest symbolic "War Prize" of the revolution and *the turning point of the war*. (These and other Troiana renditions are available on-line at https://www.wbritain.com/)

The kiosk photos below were taken at the Keller Interpretive Center at the Abingdon Muster Grounds site in Southwest Virginia. The park is part of the Overmountain Victory National Historic Trail, passing 330 miles through four states. At the time of this battle, Washington County encompassed what is now all of far Southwest Virginia:

At 3:00 p.m. on October 7th, the patriot militia army finally caught up with Ferguson and his men. Nine hundred patriots turned their rifles against Ferguson's one thousand one hundred musket-bearing loyalists. After a fierce one-hour and five minute battle, all loyalists troops were dead, wounded, or captured, compared to fewer than 100 patriot casualties. The positions on the mountain and weaponry proved to greatly benefit the patriots. Ferguson was shot dead during the battle, leaving Cornwallis without a suitable leader for the vital frontier, and consequently keeping North Carolina and Virginia out of British control.

ABINGDON MUSTER GROUNDS, VIRGINIA
The Virginia patriot militia departed from Abingdon, Virginia on September 24, 1780. There were approximately 400 men and horses from this area.

Author's Note: The National Park Service confirms above that the Battle of King's Mountain kept North Carolina and Virginia out of British control.

KILLED
Captain William Edmiston
Lieutenant Rees Bowen
Lieutenant William Blackburn
Lieutenant Robert Edmiston, S
Ensign Andrew Edmiston
Ensign Humberson Lyon
Ensign James Laird
Private William Flower
Ensign John Beattie
Ensign James Corry
Ensign Nathaniel Dryden
Ensign Nathaniel Gist
Ensign James Phillips
Ensign Thomas McCulloch
Private Elisha Pepper
Private Henry Henniger

WOUNDED
Captain James Dysart
Lieutenant Samuel Newell
Lieutenant Robert Edmiston, Jr.
Private Frederick Fisher
Private John Scaggs
Private Benoni Benning
Private Charles Kilgore
Private William Bullen
Private Leonard Hyce
Private Israel Hayter
Private William Moore

Washington County Patriots

Washington County Patriots killed and wounded at Kings Mountain. This photo was taken at the Keller Interpretive Center at the Abingdon Muster Grounds site. The site is part of the Overmountain Victory National Historic Trail, passing 330 miles through four states. At the time of this battle, Washington County encompassed what is now all of far Southwest Virginia.

Author's Note: Private Charles Kilgore was one of the five Kilgore brothers who helped defeat Ferguson's forces. Charles's brother Robert is the direct ancestor of the Kilgore population in far Southwest Virginia.

In January of the next year, 300 regular American soldiers, along with 740 Virginian and other frontier militiamen, decisively defeated

English forces at the Battle of Cowpens in South Carolina, about 40 miles from King's Mountain.

The Patriots, led by General Daniel Morgan, borrowed tactics from the King's Mountain playbook that included strategic retreats which led to ambushing opponents by way of flanking the enemy at the precise time to maximize confusion and slaughter among the opposing forces.

All in all, 800 of Lt. Colonel Tarleton's 1,000-man Redcoat soldiers were killed or captured. Tarleton, a very arrogant and sadistic military commander, was last seen riding his high horse as fast as he could in full retreat as his men lay dead, wounded, or captured.

Morgan's battle tactics were much superior to the straight-ahead English assault. He pulled off a rarely executed "double envelopment," which is a pincer movement that attacks both of the enemy's flanks at the same time. As a primer, the Overmountain Men executed a daring 360-degree multi-flank attack as they advanced up King's Mountain from all directions. Morgan lost only 25 men, with another 124 wounded.

The new country's ragtag citizen soldiers and hickory-tough back-woodsmen bested the world's best-trained and tried soldiers of that time, by a long shot. Together, the Appalachians racked up a 10:1 kill ratio at King's Mountain, and a mix of regular and mountain troops achieved a 4:1 ratio at Cowpens. Morgan also took hundreds of British soldiers out of the field of combat as prisoners; literally these two battles took away more than half of Cornwallis' original ground forces by death, debilitating wounds, or capture.

And this was not Morgan's first rodeo with the British. He was previously a wagoner for the Redcoats in the war against the French and Indians. Being somewhat thin-skinned, this American gladiator took great umbrage at being slapped by the broad side of an English officer's sword. After knocking his superior out with one punch, Morgan received 499 lashes (the flogger miscounted the 500 ordered licks), nearly killing him.

Apparently Morgan did have thin skin, plus hundreds of scars and a long memory, so the Revolutionary War gave him a chance to prove just how irritated he was. Prior to Cowpens, battlefield.com gives

Morgan this praise (paraphrased by this author): "He marched a company of crack riflemen from (western) Virginia to New England in just 21 days. His southern forces gained a reputation for fighting hard and shooting straight. The British Regulars were intimidated by these killers dressed in hunting shirts."

But Morgan's earlier southern foray into northern battlegrounds was just a whiff of what was to come home to the English.

After the Cowpens beatdown, General Cornwallis subsequently won a lesser battle against the Patriots at Greensboro, but took so many casualties among his dwindling army that he had to abandon the South. That is called a resounding defeat and a retreat in all reputable history circles except for one, as revealed below.

The spiffy Redcoat commander had lost too much, so he mustered his survivors to chase elusive Patriot units northward. He then, in a rare smart decision, gave up any idea of capturing the South. Rather, he pushed his beleaguered troops toward their eventual Waterloo at Yorktown, Virginia.

Ironically, Cornwallis' defeat and surrender to General Washington on October 19, 1781, was almost one year to the day after the Tory defeat at King's Mountain. These southern victories were very timely; Washington's northern forces during years 1779 through early 1781 were mostly unpaid, malnourished, despondent, and freezing—conditions which caused many of his troops to desert, including at least three organized mutinies. After some of the mutinous ringleaders were captured, Washington commanded their own comrades to kill them via firing squad, while other select leaders of the sustained insurrections were hanged.

In other words, the Revolution was in deep peril until teed-off Appalachians got involved. Think it through; while Washington was reduced to killing his own desperate men, mountain Patriots were mowing down Tories and Redcoats.

Yes, this enormous pre-meditated slight toward Appalachians requires a remedy. By warping history to its liking, the History Channel insults all Appalachians and our ancestors. Its series about the "Revolutionary War" carries nary a peep about the Battle of King's Mountain and how it paved the way for future non-traditional battle strategies that subdued the Tories and ultimately drove the British from the South.

These southern victories literally cleared the way for our fledgling nation to win the War of Independence. This is particularly evident by the fact that the entire American southern army was killed or captured in and around Charleston just months before the Overmountain Men swooped down to save the day.

Just as today, Appalachian military heroes are the Rodney Dangerfield of America (for younger readers, this iconic comedian made millions saying "I don't get no respect" so check him out on YouTube).

Here is the clear and convincing proof against a very biased history source. In the award-winning series *Washington*, the History Channel had this to say about Cornwallis:

"General Charles Cornwallis, who spent most of the last two years in the Carolinas, is now *moving* to Virginia. General Cornwallis is one of the *ablest* British generals, is quick-minded, he moves aggressively (and) knows how to handle troops in the field. Lord Cornwallis 'DECIDED' to go to Virginia."

Then the program's narrator goes on to deep dive into Cornwallis's wigged, snow white head and came up with this quote he divined that the British faux juggernaut was likely musing: "Virginia is home to Washington, home to Jefferson, all those patriot leaders. If I can make them suffer maybe I can get the Patriots to come to terms."

Somebody please gift the History Channel bigwigs with a Google account. They portray Cornwallis as a worthy adversary and brilliant military leader when, in fact, he was beaten like a drum as he ventured north toward the North Carolina and Virginia mountains.

According to these dubious history experts this stuffy, overrated English military leader arose from his plush bed one fine day, draped himself in a silk leisure robe, looked around and said to his attaché, "My work here is done; I have conquered everything in my sight, except for a few barbarians from the mountains, and so it is I shall leave on my own accord, in a daring fashion, and finish off the American riffraff at Yorktown."

Once again, a biased media and some highly credentialed erstwhile "historians" simply will not give credit to the South, much less Appalachians, for literally saving the all but defeated American cause.

In two masterful battles at the upper reaches of South Carolina, Washington went from almost certain defeat in the North (as his troops struggled to survive), to an ultimate victory served up on a bloody platter by Patriots from the South. Because of these battles our future president received the only good news he had heard during the grimmest part of the war.

This is what Washington knew, but apparently never fully gave proper credit for: Within a three month and two week period the Overmountain Men killed Major Ferguson and slaughtered, humiliated, and forever quelled the Tories. In doing so they paved the way for Cowpens which reversed the British occupation of the South and forced a befuddled and naïve general into Virginia to, within months, meet his ultimate defeat.

Why was Cornwallis so deathly afraid after these two stupendous defeats, to the point that he did not even try to go back to Charleston after his token win at Greensboro? To ultimately conquer the South, he knew that not a single Redcoat, including him, would come out alive if they chose to penetrate the Appalachian Mountains where the world's best marksmen lay in wait, coiled like a serpent.

Moreover, these mountain-bred human fighting machines obviously did not mind traveling south hundreds of miles by foot and horseback, in rugged terrain, to kill or capture every Tory and Redcoat they encountered. But more importantly, the Overmountain Men showed the new nation how to kill the other side, deflate their egos and spirit, and pile up the dead. They were not interested in any Marquess of Queensberry-type rules of engagement.

I can only assume that the producers and directors of these History Channel farces believe that they hold more knowledge of the War than numerous objective military sources, including three presidents of the United States and an English general (and boss of Cornwallis) who personally felt the impact.

In this era of political (and I hope historical) correctness I challenge the History Channel to right this bigotry and tell its audiences how the War was really won.

Football games are routinely won by big plays executed late in the game by a trailing team; the history of our nation is no different. The southern Patriots won the day with outstanding leadership, inspiration, guts, and skills. Mountain men, by any measure, directly caused the ultimate English retreat.

With greatly naive anticipation I look forward to the new History Channel series: "How the Battles of King's Mountain and Cowpens Won the Revolutionary War."

The truth shall set them free.

BONUS SECTIONS

GIVING PRESIDENT CARTER A JAR
OF HONEY FROM HONEY BRANCH

Note: The author has written a much more detailed book regarding the geological, natural, and human history of the Virginia Coalfields and beyond. The soon-to-be published thick copy will feature many short stories relevant to growing up in the hardscrabble Appalachian coalfields during the 1950-70 era. The following story is but one of many recollections of a real mountaineer, not a fake hillbilly.

Thanks!

I was born and raised in a holler (hollow) named Honey Branch. It is a five mile long very narrow suburb of maybe 200 residents between St. Paul and Dante, Virginia. In the 1950s and 1960s, nearly every household there, and elsewhere in our coalfield region, a World War II veteran resided. He likely worked in the coal mines, a tipple, prep plant, drove a coal truck, worked for the railroad, or logged. They were tough, tough, men and did not brook much nonsense. Our cousin, Virginia Kilgore, was only one of two women in the whole county of Wise to join the Women's Army Corps (WACS). We were very proud of her.

One wartime deserter lived at the head of the holler and no one respected him. Except, occasionally, he and my Dad (also a vet, honorably discharged) would make moonshine whiskey together.

Allen deserted the U.S. Army after his brother was killed at the Battle of the Bulge and just prior to being shipped out to Europe himself. He lived in the woods above his parents' house in a lean-to during the warm months and in an old "dog hole" abandoned coal mines in the winter. Therein he enjoyed 54-degree temperatures, plenty of water, and total darkness.

His Mom would place food out on her back porch every day or so, and he would slip down at night and take it back to his hideouts. After the war was over, he got careless and started staying in the relatively cozy family home a night or two a week.

The military police knew how to catch most deserters that were scouting, a term sometimes used for AWOLS that hid out in the big cities, thick woods, bayous, and deserts throughout America. After a couple of months passed by, the M.P.s would simply watch "Momma's house." Sooner or later the frightened absconder would make a mistake.

Allen was thus captured and dishonorably discharged after doing time in the brig and watching his uniform burn in front of fellow soldiers. He never held a real job, rarely took a bath, and was pretty nasty in speech and habit all around. The other vets I knew were proud, supported their family, voted in every election, and kept the same job until they retired. "Solid as a rock" described them to a tee.

The name "Honey Branch" inspired me later in life in a situation I could not have imagined while growing up in a hardscrabble world. My Dad raised honeybees and started his first hive from a swarm that flew around me as I was wading up the creek, looking for muskrats to trap. The swarm, I thought, was trying to land on me, so I lay down in the creek until they settled around the queen in a big willow tree branch overhead. Dad caught them and started his own honeybee colony.

As the colony repeatedly exiled the next queen and swarm, he added more bee boxes until we had a dozen or so in a big bee village on the steep hillside overlooking our small, drafty frame house. We had fresh honey and comb to spare.

Years later, while attending Clinch Valley College (an off-campus extension of the University of Virginia) I met a sociology professor named Helen Lewis. I signed up for an Appalachian Seminar night class she taught while I was working full time and starting a family. I took college very seriously, unlike high school. My professors were impressed that I worked full-time while attending college full-time. It never occurred to me that I had a choice.

Dr. Lewis suggested that I start a citizens' group of local people to push for better strip mining reclamation laws as a class project. At that time Virginia was dead last in the nation when it came to regulating this very earth-shattering coal mining method. Little did she know that I would take my mission to heart so zealously nor did either of us fathom that my activities would later end her job.

Years later, as she was delivering somewhat of a returned exile homecoming speech at the college, I learned for the first time that the dozen or so students prior to me she had suggested take on this project never did a thing; apparently I thought it was an honor to have a "doctor" express confidence in me. She is in her nineties now and resides in a nursing home and, until COVID, I frequently visited her with food and thanks.

The problem was real, however. Coal companies could mine within five feet of their neighbors' property lines. They sometimes blasted rocks through the roofs of buildings including the gymnasium and covered pool at our college. Dynamite and ammonia nitrate powered explosions cracked house foundations and one mega blast registered on the Richter Scale over 120 air miles away at Virginia Tech. One company rolled a Volkswagen-sized rock onto the Norton Elementary School playground. And that was just in my little part of coalfield Appalachia.

Several private cemeteries were disturbed, and mining near secondary public roads caused landslides and collapsed shoulders while overloaded coal trucks busted pavement and spilled coal dust onto the roads by the tons. Creeks were filled with uprooted trees, rocks, dirt, and silt to the point that local flooding was frequent and aquatic life rare.

It was as if free-range Hell's Angels had been provided bulldozers, augers, drills, and dynamite instead of Harleys.

Local resistance toward proposed federal mining restrictions was fierce in many powerful circles as I took my slideshow (now called PowerPoint) on the road. The color photos depicted muddy streams, huge landslides, blasted homes, and soaring high walls to the dozens of civic groups, schools, and public hearings that allowed me in. Things sometimes got tense.

I was often the only person in a packed room or auditorium openly and loudly supporting the proposed federal surface-mining act. I was routinely threatened, and in one incident a carload of men in a black Torino tried to run me off of Wise Mountain road as I drove home from my wrestling coach night job at the Job Corps. After the driver tried to ram my small pickup from behind, I swerved over to a wide spot, stopped, and vigorously exercised my right of self-defense. Tires squealed and smoke spewed out of the tailpipe as the slick muscle car sped away.

They returned the favor a few months later on Christmas Eve as I was loading presents into my pickup truck to take my children to visit their maternal grandparents. Always wary, I noticed the same car speed by my dirt driveway as an arm stretched from a side window. Very soon a hand gun barked three times. Bullets whizzed overhead into the nearby trees. For some reason neither incident surprised me, but I do believe they were not expecting a "tree hugger" to stand his ground.

I was, after all, an Appalachian redneck 'tree-hugger' with one consistent motto: let bullies know there are consequences.

An advocacy group I founded in 1975, the Virginia Citizens for Better Reclamation (VCBR), became nationally known because of our coalfield roots and persistence. Our membership was mostly made up of United Mine Workers underground miners, blasting victims, the occasional homegrown conservationist, and a few "outsiders" that came to appreciate our mountains. Back then we natives mostly took our ancient, biologically diverse hills for granted.

VCBR was also known, and begrudgingly respected at times, for not advocating the abolition of strip mining. This position caused many national environmental groups to shun or verbally attack us (once in a D.C. church). In other words, we equally enraged both extreme sides of the issue.

This experience taught me that only lazy or stupid people pursue an "all-or-nothing" position on important issues. Getting nothing is not too smart, and those that get it usually quit trying to do anything positive.

The federal law had already passed Congress once, but President Gerald Ford vetoed it and a vote to override him fell short. Then Jimmy Carter took office and promised to sign the bill if it got to his desk. We went to work even harder.

After kicking off the initial congressional hearings with my slideshow before the House Natural Resource Committee, chaired by Congressman Morris Udall, I was very pleased to see that progress was being made. As I walked down the steps of the Capitol, after completely debunking the industry's fake reclamation presentations, a coal operator (and "high-powered" lawyer) and two of his big truck driver escorts confronted me on the city sidewalk. I was told in a stern, patronizing voice what was surely going to happen to me when I got "back home."

The lawyer was upset that Congress just viewed authentic photos of strip mining abuse instead of the doctored photos circulated by him and the mining lobbyists that showed happy cattle dining on thickly grassed strip mines.

That particular photographed site they handed out was two miles from my small, rented house. The "pasture" did not have a fence around it. The cattle had been unloaded from a livestock trailer, the serene pictures taken, then the bovines were loaded back up. That expose', plus my undoctored pictures of holes in the roofs of houses, the damaged college gymnasium and swimming pool, 300 to 400 feet long landslides, mud-laden creeks, and spilled coal covering public roads were potent.

So, just as I was feeling my oats there I was, on the streets of Washington, D.C. being threatened again. I responded just as the Over Mountain men did during the Revolutionary War when Major Patrick Ferguson threatened to invade their mountain homes with fire and sword if they didn't cower down to England and stay home. I became proactive.

"Why wait until we get home!!?" I shouted at the lawyer. His two burly friends stood frozen on either side, their eyes widening as I stepped forward.

"Let's do it right here, one at a time, and see who gets home!" I screamed.

This was apparently not the response they expected, and I saw that I had the momentum. So I stepped even closer toward them with clenched fists, truly ready to jack the very jaw that spurted the next word.

Just then a friend who had accompanied me to D.C. ran back across the street and grabbed my cocked arm. When he first saw a fight developing he had wisely left the scene, thinking I would follow his lead.

"Frank," he shouted, "you're a young, well-fed, good-looking country boy, you do not want to be locked up in a D.C. jail tonight!" It was not often back then that such clarity and visual perceptions ran through my brain during tense confrontations, but his words were impressive. (He later became a big and small-time screen actor).

Not one to leave well enough alone, I told my main nemesis that *he* would be in trouble when *I* got back home. Sure enough, months later our group caused him to be indicted in federal court for re-channeling a river flowing through the City of Norton without a permit.

It has been an oddity throughout my life that when bullies threaten me, their turn on the hot seat swings into view sooner or later. Karma is inexplicable, assuming there is such a mysterious force.

After I started practicing law a few years later, the same legendary attorney who'd confronted me on the street in Washington and I made each other as miserable as possible. He sued me with frivolous claims, and I nailed him once for being intoxicated while trying a jury case that he lost. It was time-consuming, but many times gratifying. Thirty years later we finally buried the hatchet as his health declined and, ironically, he needed me to come to his aid to save his law license due to some specious accusations. I took my lawyer oath seriously and told the truth, which happened to be in his favor.

We had harassed each other over the years until it became pointless. He was a court room warrior, steam-roller, and a true colorful mountain character. I cannot say I was ever personally fond of him, but time and experience has taught me to sometimes see humor instead of rage when it comes to the human condition. But I digress, greatly.

After the aforesaid sidewalk confrontation, I soon found myself back in Washington, D.C., appearing before the U.S. Senate as the federal strip mining bill kept moving forward. I later accompanied members of the House and Senate on a helicopter tour above the strip mines of Southwest Virginia. They were speechless at what they saw.

During the flyover I sat next to Chairman Udall as we approached a strip-mining site where dozens of landslides extended hundreds of feet down slope before slamming into streams near the Wise airport. The coal operator, Jerry, was there to explain this undeniable carnage by stating that his company was new at strip mining and they didn't realize what would happen.

I cut him off abruptly and asked him if he was aware of the laws of physics, particularly gravity. He turned very red-faced. Then I pointed out that his father started the first strip mine in Wise County in 1948. I then wondered very out loud "just how was it" by the 1960s and 70s they had not learned these laws of physics since surely there were no state laws to learn, etc.

I was on a roll, assuming that my personal safety was assured by the U.S. Government.

Jerry was furious, and we edged closer to each other, "bowed up" to the max. Chairman Udall called us down and got on the helicopter to leave. When I started to climb on board he said, for the first time, that he and his entourage were flying directly to West Virginia next. He suggested that I could catch a ride with one of "those gentlemen," one being the coal operator I just fricasseed on his own property, and the other a state mining inspector who just heard me call his agency a coal industry lap dog.

After climbing up a collapsed highwall to avoid having to ask anyone for a favor, especially a hostile, I started walking east toward my home, a mere 20 miles away.

The state inspector waited until Jerry left as I topped the ridge above the high wall before shouting at me: "Get your hillbilly butt down here!"

I sheepishly climbed into the state Jeep with the inspector, who laughed at my predicament but finally conceded that his agency had its hands tied due to the coal industry's political might in Richmond.

He basically agreed to my lap dog theory and later became a top-notch federal strip mine inspector.

What I didn't realize during the drama was that the *Washington Post* photographer accompanying us had climbed the highwall after me and photographed the helicopter sitting on the strip mine bench with a background of landslides and waste as far as the camera could capture. I was in the forefront of the photo, looking lean, determined, and clueless.

The photo and Sunday article about the federal act made it onto the front page above the crease, further cementing among the coal industry that I was solely to blame for slowing down their ransacking of coalfield Appalachia. Obviously I was not the sole reason the bill passed. But "back home" I was the native son who saw things much differently than the industry-dominated political and social cultures that prospered the most from "shoot and shove" strip mining.

Va. Strip Mining Brings Prosperity, Woes
by Paul G. Edwards
July 31, 1977
(reprinted with permission)

From a helicopter fluttering through the hot haze over Virginia's Cumberland Mountains 325 miles southwest of Washington, the passenger can watch the good and bad effects of the region's coal boom real past below.

In the streets of Wise and Norton towns that declined for 25 years during the regional recession that made Appalachia synonymous with hard times, coal trucks and late model automobiles pass in a steady stream. New housing dots the hillsides around the towns and the main roads are lined with the low, steel structures that house the office of surface mine operators and heavy equipment dealers.

The banks that once occupied the ground floors of aging red brick buildings in town centers now stand out as scattered, new structures on the edge of black parking lots.

Everywhere, the shiny outlets of the fast food chains suggest a rising personal disposable income in an area where family nutrition long relied on food stamps and garden plots.

These are the signs of prosperity, but even a brief helicopter flight also shows that this prosperity arrived at a cost.

Northwest of Wise, the steep slopes of Little Black Mountain lie bare, stripped of the hardwood forests that slopes are covered with the rocky rubble that was ripped away to reach the thin seams of coal that run through the mountain.

On the edge of Norton, the still raw site of a complete hilltop mine reaches to within a few feet of the back doors of the modest home on 13th Street.

One of the 13th Street residents, retired coal miner, Ewin Davison, 65, said in an interview that the dust created by the months-long strip mining operation covered the neighborhood so thickly that his 14-year-old son, Jeffrey Lynn, contracted silicosis.

Davidson also said blasting at the mine site broke windows and cracked the chimney of his home and sent rocks flying through the roofs of at least two houses in the area.

About two blocks away on Park Avenue, Norton's main streets, Mrs. Joseph Fischer showed visitors what she said was damage caused to her 12-year-old brick home by strip mine blasting. It included a four-foot crack in the block walls of the basement and wide separations between the basement floor and walls.

Most of the strip mines, of course, are located in lightly populated rural areas, but the mines also have caused complaints. In small communities of Lee County near Pennington Gap, residents contend that recent flooding of their low-lying homes was caused by rapid runoff from stripped areas high on the mountainsides.

Mud covered roads in front of the homes and buried tomato plants and other vegetables in their garden, they said, as the heavy rains of late spring carried slit away from the mine sites.

Against this background of prosperity and grievances - both stimulated by strip mining - some dramatic developments are occurring in Virginia's coal-fields.

For the first time, a citizens organization of coal field residents - the still small but rapidly growing Virginia Citizens for Better Reclamation (VCBR) - is increasing pressure for local, state and federal government controls on mining.

At the same time, the state agency that regulates strip mining is about to impose significantly more stringent regulations on mining methods and Congress is near enactment of even tougher federal strip mine restraints.

There continues to be fierce debates over how effective these proposed regulations will be in limiting the adverse effects of strip mining. There also are questions about how much they will add to the price of coal, a major factor in rising electric bills.

In Virginia, these debates are developing what appear to the last years of the controversial strip mining industry. According to figures recently published by the state planning district commissions in the coal fields, strip mine production in Virginia should total 12.4 million tons this year, about one-third of the state's total coal production.

It is projected to decline steadily until 1990 when Virginia's surface mine reserves are expected to be depleted. By then, all of Virginia's coal will come from deep mines, from which production is projected to rise from about 26 million tons this year to 60 million tons by 1990.

But before the strip mining era ends in Virginia, the planning commissions' surveys predict that about 127 square miles in seven counties will have been disturbed. This would be roughly 8 per cent of the region in which the mines are located. The majority of this area, about 75 square miles, already was mined by 1975, the surveys showed.

There appear to be three explanations for the pressure for tougher strip mine regulations so late in the day of strip mining in Virginia. One is that mining activity increased rapidly after the 1973 Arab Oil embargo and attracted more complaints. Another is that Virginia strip mining is occurring at a time of proposed federal regulation of a growing nationwide industry.

The third reason appears to be Frank Kilgore, a 25-year-old descendant of 18th century Irish settlers of Southwest Virginia and the founder of VCBR, Kilgore, the son and grandson of coal miners, lives with his wife and two children in Honey Branch hollow near the town of St. Paul on the eastern edge of Virginia's coal fields.

He understands as well as anyone why it has taken so long for anyone to start a movement for improved strip mine reclamation practices in Southwest Virginia, a part of the country that tends to resist advice from "outsiders."

"People just don't have the effectiveness in getting the government to act in this area that they do in other places," he said in an interview. "Looking down here - rocks through the roofs of houses and silicosis from the dust created by strip mining."

Kilgore said he has wanted to work for strip mine controls ever since he was about 12 years old and first saw the results of strip mining on hunting trips with his father near Honey Branch.

He organized VCBR and put together a slide show used to promote the organization in 1976 on a Southern Appalachian leadership grant. The organization, he said, has been financed during the first 18 months of its activities on grants totaling $18,000 from the Ford Foundation and churches.

Kilgore said he has been the target of threats and assaults since he began his campaign for strip mine controls. He said someone in a passing car fired a shot at him last Christmas Eve as he stood in the yard of his home. The driver of what appeared to him to be the same car also tried to force him off a mountainous road one night as he drove home from nearby Wise.

Nevertheless, Kilgore said VCBR has steadily grown to 350

members and is gaining influence partly because it is based in the coal fields and includes coal miners.

"At least people are talking in the open about better reclamation of mined land." he said. "That has never happened down here before."

Kilgore says the organization does not oppose strip mining - "That would be ridiculous in the coal fields" - but advocates regulations that would prevent pushing spoil (land stripped from above the coal seam) down the mountainsides and reduce erosion that fills coal field streams with silt.

VCBR also is working for tighter regulation of blasting that would prevent the kind of damage reported by Norton residents. Kilgore said that Edward S. Grandis, VCBR's only full time employee, has drafted major provisions restricting blasting that is contained in the federal legislation.

"I hate to see the federal government take over strip mining regulation" Kilgore said, "but the state has taken a hands-off policy. The basic provisions in the federal bill couldn't be passed in Virginia in 20 years."

Surface mine operators have strongly, opposed the federal bill. Some of them have claimed that a provision requiring operators to restore stripped land to its original contour would end strip mining in Virginia because of the steep slopes in its coal fields.

However, James A. Brown Jr., one of the most successful coal operators in Wise County, believes that stripping will continue under the federal bill-but at a higher price to consumers and with higher profits for operators.

"You can do anything in the way of reclamation that the public will pay for in higher coal prices," he said in an interview. "We make 20 per cent before taxes on each ton of coal. We make 20 per cent of $22 now. If the federal government adds to the price of coal through reclamation costs, we'll make 20 per cent of the higher price."

Brown estimates that the federal legislation would add about $6 a ton to the price surface mine coal now selling for $22. "That's about a mid-range estimate." he said. "The conservationists say much less and the real pessimists say much more."

Brown said he generally supports efforts to reduce strip mine erosion that fills streams and reservoirs with silt, but believes that much in the proposed state and federal regulations are unnecessary and may even contribute to erosion.

"I don't think we should add to the price of coal for things that are not needed," he said. "If the government simply added a $4 a ton tax on coal instead of adding to reclamation costs and then decided how it should spend the tax money. I don't think it would spend it for the things being required in the federal bill. It would spend it on the things we need, like roads, schools and energy research."

[end of article]

I received a call a few days before the law was being signed by President Jimmy Carter in the White House Rose Garden. I had made friends with one moderate national environmental group, and the director had gotten me an invitation to attend. I was excited but nearly penniless. Every cent I earned was spoken for. I grossed about $130.00 per week. So VCBR's membership passed the hat and raised enough "gas money" to see me off to the nation's capital, where I "stayed all night" with my hostess and her husband.

The next day we entered the White House unsearched. In those days security was lax, and the strapping Secret Service agents were friendly and welcoming. That was about to change.

My first disappointment was that the plan for me to stand near the President as he signed this landmark legislation was changed at the last minute. I was the only coalfield resident at the event, my hostess informed me, so Congressman Udall wanted me front and center.

As we were being lined up by the White House photographer, he evidently noticed my green tee shirt and blue jeans. Not having any "dress up" clothes, I figured that Jimmy, a peanut farmer after all, would not mind. The photographer felt differently.

He stuck me in the third row, where my shirt and pants would not spoil his otherwise perfect photo of 1970s suits and dresses worn by what I assumed were very rich people. Only my bushy hair, high cheekbone, and one brown beady eye were visible in the photo. But that slight turned out to be a relatively minor setback.

ALTHOUGH IT WAS August and very hot, I had a light jacket draped over my arm. Under it was a quart of my Dad's honey and on a piece of masking tape in all caps I hand-wrote: "HONEY FROM HONEY BRANCH, VIRGINIA FOR JIMMY CARTER (and his family)".

I was amazed how clever this would be and envisioned that when I went through the line to shake the President's hand I would whip out the jar of honey and present it to him. Of course he would then read the label out loud. Then, the next morning, the President of the United States of America would sit at the White House kitchen table and share the sweet contents with Rosalynn and Amy over hot buttered "cathead" biscuits. I was set.

Everything was going great while shaking the President's hand as Chairman Udall bent down to tell him about my role in supporting the Act. Then I pulled out my gift and "reached" the honey jar toward the President. The now un-friendly Secret Service agents jumped forward to grab this gift of appreciation, but I was too quick.

I recoiled and backed the several feet onto the Rose Garden portico and would not let go of the treasure. When one of the agents grabbed my forearm I "bowed up," a common defensive (and offensive) measure well-meaning rednecks often employ when befuddled.

I suppose I was a split second away from either being knocked out or shot (or both) when my red-faced hostess ran toward us screaming.

"Wait, wait, wait, I know him, I know him! Let me handle it!"

The agents let her slip between them, and she calmly asked me what the problem might be. I explained my surprise gift for the President and showed her the jar and label. She said that was a "real sweet" thing to do, which I thought was a pun thing to say about honey so I laughed a little.

She then promised to make sure the President received the gift. I surrendered it to her and "eyeballed" the agents one last time before leaving the White House, proud and oblivious, but upright.

I am pretty sure, in hindsight, that the honey from Honey Branch probably never made it to the Carter family's breakfast table.

UNSOLICITED ADVICE FROM AN OWG REGARDING CURRENT ISSUES OF INTEREST

THE POLICE

Underpaid, yes; under-trained, yes; under-appreciated, yes; too many violations of your oath to protect and serve the public, yes. Your oath to stop and/or arrest anyone violating the law has no exceptions. If you see the police breaking the law, it's your duty to stop and/or arrest him or her then and there. If no one is above the law, that includes out-of-control colleagues. Do this one thing consistently and public trust will follow. Decent citizens appreciate 90% of you, but only you can police the minority of officers with guns, badges, and toxic attitudes. I was in law enforcement back in the day, the bad eggs make sure they stand out. Do not cover up their crimes; they are criminals when they break the law. You know who they are.

DEFUND THE POLICE ADVOCATES

Move into a high-crime area, then refuse to call the police when someone breaks into your residence with a gun. Call a social worker. One more thing, don't speak for impoverished high-crime neighborhoods unless you live there. The actual residents there may very well have a different opinion, such as protecting their family.

WOKE CROWD

Are you an agent for needed reform? Sure, you could be, history is full of beneficial agents of change. It could be argued that our

Founding Fathers were woke. After all, they risked their property and lives to create a new nation. The English, by the way, were fervent proponents of hanging "traitors." To now judge Washington, Jefferson, Monroe, Adams, and other Founders in the light of current standards is a lazy hit job. And attacking Grant and Lincoln? That's why your favorite politicians are having second thoughts about your support. Who's next, Martin Luther King for his alleged misogynist behavior? If you cancel him and Thomas Jefferson, then no one is safe and thousands of streets and schools will have to be renamed. Were these men flawed? Of course, all humans are, particularly Jefferson it seems. But they all risked everything to create what has over the centuries become a beacon of democracy. So, assuming you are not laying your life and assets on the line as they did, you lose your credibility when you equate personal peeves with the common good. It's fair game to expose the settled facts about anyone, particularly our great leaders past and present, but to erase the good they have done is so Russian.

WARPED RELIGIOUS BELIEFS

If you are willing to kill people due to a difference of religious beliefs, you might not be all that religious. Not many faiths condone murder.

POLITICS

If you hate someone just because he or she doesn't agree with your political beliefs, then you should turn in your USA card. We fought the British to have freedom of thought and association. Many American soldiers have died since then to guarantee these liberties. Move to Cuba if you want a society where average citizens have lost the freedom of expression. It's not that far away, many Americans will chip in for your voyage.

PEDOPHILES AND THEIR ENABLERS

They both are sick with little chance of being cured. If the decent citizens among us know or reasonably suspect that a child is being molested, we should not rest until the authorities do something about it. Doing nothing is for cowards and enablers. Is that how these purposely blind, selfish, pitiful wimps want to leave this world? Letting children be forever scarred by saying nothing? Surely not.

AT-RISK CHILDREN

They may have never heard a kind or encouraging word from a

respected adult. Providing that simple and sometimes life-changing gift costs nothing. Don't be naive about saving them all, unfortunately most humans are "set in their ways" by our mid-teens. But there are exceptions; find them.

"WORK" IS NOT A DIRTY FOUR-LETTER WORD

Work. Do what you can to have a purposeful life. Whether it's a full-time paying job, visiting the elderly and veterans, or helping a child in need, do something. Pick up litter, work at food banks, help your Momma, something to show an appreciation for life. If all else fails, write a book. Imagine on your deathbed the only thing your family and friends can come up with is, "He sure liked watching TV, playing video games, and eating hot dogs." If that's the sum total of your presence here on this earth, what a pity. People who say "there is nothing to do around here" ain't looking very hard.

DO NOT CHASE PEOPLE UNLESS YOU ARE THE POLICE (OR PLAYING FOOTBALL)

What did the Ahmaud Arbey murder and the Kyle Rittenhouse shootings teach us? Don't chase people who are desperate to get away from you unless you are the police or a linebacker; juries don't like that.

PARTING THOUGHTS FROM A REAL MOUNTAINEER
MOVE TO COALFIELD APPALACHIA

Dear Beleaguered Americans: I welcome you to move to coalfield Appalachia.

Want to avoid extreme weather, killer gangs, and excessive wokeness? Live in central coalfield Appalachia. No raging forest fires, no hurricanes, no extreme droughts, no riots, no smothering taxes, no traffic gridlocks, and no killer tornadoes. Flood damages are avoidable, rainfall plentiful, wildlife teeming, biodiversity everywhere, land affordable, outdoor recreation abundant, police and military respected, strangers accommodated, patriotism honored, primary roads excellent, and high-speed internet available along most major corridors. Last but not least, differing opinions are welcomed, except talking violence-laced smack against our country and flag.

Your qualifications? Bring or create good jobs here, be a good neighbor, and come ready for peace of mind.

Job creators: for a tour you won't forget, email info@FakeHillbilly-Publishing.com.

ONE MORE THING OR TWO:
BOTTOM-LINE HUMAN RIGHTS

The most basic human right worldwide is being able to defend yourself and loved ones against killers, robbers, rapists, and molesters. Rich people with body guards and residents of gated, guarded, or otherwise low-crime communities have no standing to preach to anyone about giving up that right.

Another human right for free-thinking adults is to go out of this life how and when we wish, as long as that does not involve taking non-consenting people out with us. The government, clergy, and public policy influencers should have no say in what consenting, full-grown adults wish to do in our waning years. Death with dignity sure beats being slowly eaten alive by some insidious fatal disease, lying in a burn center for months or years, or being in a drug-induced stupor at an adult facility, listening to high-volume daytime TV. Checking out should be each individual's choice and business, period.

Most importantly, the right to live is also a pretty compelling human right. Of all the people who should demand red flag laws to deal with potential mass murderers, it should be law-and-order gun owners like me and hundreds of my kin and friends. I don't get it; how can this be a big government intrusion as alleged by the far right? I expected a push back from the liberal left and was gob smacked to hear this pitifully weak argument coming from gun owner organizations.

If someone is brazen and crazy enough to post or verbalize their desire to kill other human beings, such self-illumination cannot be ignored. There are no Constitutional barriers to having these folks taken off the street until a due process work-up is done and the matter legally investigated. Most states already have some form of due process system to have people exhibiting mental health symptoms detained and evaluated. The red flag process simply takes emergency aim at the hallucinating gun owners, or potential gun buyers, amongst the relatively non-violent troubled folks with a garden variety of treatable fantasies and abnormal traits.

How many times do we have to hear and see that other people, including parents for crying out loud, notified the police or school officials that a sick relative is promising and planning a killing spree? Then no action is taken. Some folks say it's profiling to engage these deranged wanna-be killers early on to see if they will incriminate themselves even further. Is it profiling for law enforcement to cast a broad net for pedophiles by pretending to be an underage soft target? No!

And think about this, United States Code Title 18, Section 871, imposes a felony prosecution for threatening to kill a president of the United States; so how can that same type of state law not be constitutionally available to other citizens who are being threatened by a potential killer that can access us 24/7 as we attend schools, churches and malls? The arguments against properly worded red flag laws are bogus.

Nor is it entrapment when self-proclaimed violent aggressors take the bait for something they very much intend to do, most likely plotted to do in the past, and will continue fantasizing to do until locked up for their own safety and the protection of others while a mental evaluation is concluded. If further detention is provided by law and ordered by jurists after a due process hearing is completed, then that is what should be done. If nothing is done, it is literally too late for the victims who had no idea that morning that they are going to be shot later that day for simply existing.

How many random killings can we absorb without taking these nuts out of action long enough to at least figure out what to do next through the due process legal system? This refusal to protect innocent American citizens, particularly children, can't be blamed on the Woke crowd, just the uncaring crowd.

One final note and a direct message to potential mass murderers: Why do children at schools and average citizens just having a good time drive you crazy? Be a man (women rarely do this crazy stuff, so call me a sexist for leaving them out) and take on dangerous gang hangouts or call out participants at a pedophile convention. Then bare-knuckle your way out of these self-imposed predicaments and brag about it later, if you can. Leave our children alone. Just because your childhood sucked, harming kids and their loving kin will not cure your insanity. You think being smacked on the play ground only happened to you? How do you think you will feel when inmates at a super max prison have their way? That's where you are headed, should you survive.

THAT'S ALL FOLKS

21580545R00100